Money and Ideas

International Studies in Entrepreneurship

Series Editors:

Zoltan J. Acs
George Mason University
Fairfax, VA, USA

David B. Audretsch
Indiana University
Bloomington, IN, USA

For other titles published in this series, go to
http://www.springer.com/series/6149

Prashanth Mahagaonkar

Money and Ideas

Four Studies on Finance, Innovation
and the Business Life Cycle

 Springer

Prashanth Mahagaonkar
Abt. Entrepreneurship Growth and Public Policy
Max Planck Institute of Economics
Kahlaische str. 10, 07745 Jena
Germany
prashanth.mahagaonkar@gmail.com

ISBN 978-1-4419-1227-5   e-ISBN 978-1-4419-1228-2
DOI 10.1007/978-1-4419-1228-2
Springer New York Dordrecht Heidelberg London

Library of Congress Control Number: 2009940200

Printed on acid-free paper

Springer is part of Springer Science+Business Media (www.springer.com)

Preface

This is the age of start-ups and up-starts. At the same time, we are passing through a phase of financial meltdown and series of economic and geo-political uncertainties. Therefore, the central question for economic research is: how to support small firms and encourage new start-ups such that they can sustain through such volatile times? Small firms and start-ups generally face many problems with finance, especially in times of financial crises. Along with it, the problems of inherent bureaucratic regulations and banking restrictions often obstruct the growth of entrepreneurs. I tried to study these inter-related issues through this book.

In this process I have been lucky to have valuable co-authors. The first paper in this book, 'Financial Signalling by Innovative Nascent Entrepreneurs', was co-authored with Prof. David B. Audretsch and Prof. Werner Bönte. The second paper, 'What do Scientists Want: Money or Fame?', was co-authored with Dr. Devrim Goktepe-Hultén. The third paper, 'Regional Financial System and the Financial Structure of Small Firms', and the fourth, 'Corruption and Innovation: A Grease or Sand relationship?', are both solely authored by me.

These papers have been presented in prominent academic international conferences. These include, for instance, the 55th North American Regional Science Association Conference (NARSC) 2008, the annual conference of European Public Choice Society (EPCS) 2008, 3rd ZEW Conference on the Economics of Innovation and Patenting 2008 and the Danish Research Unit for Innovation Dynamics (DRUID) annual conference 2007. These papers are also published in the Jena Economic Research Papers series and the DRUID discussion papers series.

Acknowledgments

The root of the word 'thank' is the same as that of *'think'*. I am indeed fortunate to be associated with people in places where thought is placed in highest respect; where learning holds the highest post. There are many people who played a role in churning, skimming and always updating my thought-machine. My first teacher of thoughts was Sri Sathya Sai Baba who taught me that knowledge of the self is the highest form of knowledge. My first lessons in economic thought also started at the same time. The faculty of economics at Sri Sathya Sai University helped me appreciate the beauty of economics and had laid the basic foundation for my future. I express my gratitude to each of them.

This pursuit of knowledge then took me to University of Hyderabad. A new system, new challenges and a new opportunity of learning greeted me there. More than fantasizing about the beauty of economics, I had to now come to grips with its ways and language. Many teachers helped me in this process. I cannot forget Late Prof. Madduri's econometrics classes where I had learnt that a difficult subject can be dealt easily if one had a good teacher. He was also responsible for my first steps into entrepreneurship research. Without interactions with those 200 entrepreneurs, I would not have understood the problems with finance and to start thinking of solutions. My sincere gratitude also goes to Late Prof. Umashankar Patnaik who made me write the first conference paper of my life and introduced me to the world of research. The entire faculty of economics at the University of Hyderabad was responsible in my learning process in one way or the other.

While I got convinced to pursue research, Prof. K. Narayanan from IIT Bombay helped me to actually start this process - To understand the financial problems of small firms and also to understand how to do research. Later on as I learnt more I sought newer avenues of entrepreneurship research. This is when I came across the works of Prof. David Audretsch. Looking at the group's research interests, I could not but agree that the Max Planck Institute of Economics was the right place to give my knowledge-seeking, a good form. My thanks to David, for helping me develop an insightful and goal-oriented approach towards my book and for putting together such a great team to work with.

Enter autumn 2006 and I start working with Prof. Werner Bönte on a topic that we were always interested in – finance and innovation. I learnt a lot during this project and I am still learning a lot from Werner. One cannot find a better supervisor to work with. Thank you Werner for all the insights, support and of course for being my supervisor. I am sure there are many more exciting avenues to work together.

Many people are responsible for this book, of course, for all good reasons. Knowledge pursuit cannot be always done alone. I am thankful to Prof. Uwe Cantner and the members of the Graduate college of Economics of Innovation at the University of Jena who gave me exposure to the world of innovation. I am glad I have good friends and co-authors like - Aditya Sathyan, Devrim Göktepe, Swayan Chaudhuri, Jianying Qiu, Erik Monsen, Jörg Zimmermann and Diemo Urbig who are wonderful to work with.

Be it intellectual talk or having a coffee, I always find company in wonderful people like Holger Patzelt, Birendra Rai, Pawan Tamvada, Taylor Aldridge, Iris Beckmann, Stefan Krabel, Anja Klaukien, Viktor Slavtchev, Adam lederer, Stephan Heblich, Robert Gold, Robin Bürger, Madeleine Schmidt, Ute Filipiak and Kerstin Schueck. I know that no word of thanks equal your understanding and support, I am just glad that I continue to always have a good time with you all.

Any good pursuit of knowledge needs financial, technical and literary support. I thank the Max Planck Society and the administration department at the Max Planck Institute of Economics, who provided me with all the necessary financial support for my book. I really appreciate the efforts by the staff of the library who provided books in time, and also for providing with the virtual knowledge base. Thanks to you all. My research was amply supported on the technical side by the I.T. Department of the institute. I must thank them also for their patience with my requests for extra memory and providing it in time. Knowledge needs space too!

My pursuit of self-knowledge did not end in India. It continued with Jana in Germany. When in doubt, she helped me look at the brighter side- which was always the true side. I am glad that she is there. The roots of knowledge are sown by the family. I am quite grateful to my parents- Shanta and Suresh for providing me with their understanding, trust and love. I am happy to be have sisters like Uma and Sudha, who always provide the cheer. Knowledge needs cheerfulness too!

The pursuit continues.

About the author

Prashanth Mahagaonkar's interest in entrepreneurship research began with remarkable experiences while working with almost 300 small business owners in India. The word "constraint" took many forms during these interactions. While for one entrepreneur it was always an issue of finance, while for other it was marketing or how to get new technology. How do entrepreneurs face these problems? are there any economic solutions to identify and correct these problems? These were the questions that Prashanth brought with him along when he joined as a research fellow at the entrepreneurship, growth and public policy group of the Max Planck Institute of Economics, Germany. Research ideally must take the form of practice, and therefore Prashanth also studies scientists' intentions and opinions on commercialization of science. On the practice side, Prashanth's interests fall in the area of turnaround strategies, business performance, innovation and knowledge management.

Along with the issues of innovation and finance, Prashanth also works on exchange rate economics and development economics. Prashanth's work appeared in the Center for Economic Policy Reseach Paper series, Jena Economics Research Paper series as well as in peer-reviewed international journals. Prashanth is also associated with the Schumpeter School of Business and Economics in the University of Wuppertal, where he completed his PhD dissertation under the guidance of Professors Werner Bönte and David B. Audretsch.

Prashanth currently is a senior research fellow at the Entrepreneurship, Growth and Public Policy group of the Max Planck Institute of Economics in Jena, Germany. When not working, Prashanth actively engages in photography, experimental art and hiking.

Contents

List of Figures

List of Tables

Chapter 1
Introduction

> *"Today, one in three small businesses is unable to obtain finance and has seen the cost of existing finance increase dramatically"*
> *– John Wright*[1]

The current global financial crisis is difficult for small firms. Small firms face contraction of credit from banks, which affects their future investments adversely. On the equity side, there is a general lack of trust from investors due to increasing uncertainties every day. Therefore, investment in future projects using either debt or equity becomes difficult for small businesses in general.

While small firms face these difficulties, the *New York Times* (Flanigan, 2008) recently reported that entrepreneurs with innovative ideas and technologies do not face a funding gap even during the current crisis. There seems to be some hope among investors on the potential of innovations and the individuals who bring these to the market. One entrepreneur stated that in this crisis "companies cant raise debt so there are opportunities for equity investment." This investment, in his opinion, will be in areas where new technologies are constantly evolving. In short, the *New York Times* calls it the "entrepreneurial edge," which involves the innovative idea and the individual.

Has mainstream economic theory concentrated on this entrepreneurial edge? It is only after the 1930s that the role of an individual in economic process was considered important. The "individual" became the center of economic activity in models initiated by economists like Joseph A. Schumpeter and A.C. Pigou when they included psychological aspects into business cycle theories. Schumpeter considered this "individual" – the entrepreneur – as the key to the process of economic development. An entrepreneur is crucial in the process of bringing new inventions to the market, leading to successful innovations (Schumpeter, 1934, 1942). Observing the economic development of developed economies in the last three decades, one cannot but agree that Schumpeter was indeed right. The individual as well as the knowledge creation and dissemination processes play an important role in economic growth.

One of the central issues of Schumpeter's analysis was also the allocation of *financial resources*. Indeed, the entrepreneur is important but not without a proper allocation of financial resources. Schumpeter therefore emphasized the role that money markets play. Money is not only a medium to facilitate circulation of goods,

P. Mahagaonkar, *Money and Ideas: Four Studies on Finance, Innovation and the Business Life Cycle*, International Studies in Entrepreneurship 25, DOI 10.1007/978-1-4419-1228-2_1, © Springer Science+Business Media, LLC 2010

but also empowers the entrepreneur as a leverage that can initiate the process of creative destruction itself, which is the key to economic development. While a portion of this leverage comes from the entrepreneur herself, an additional push comes from external money markets. Whether it is for long-term investment, payroll, or working capital requirements, obtaining additional finances remains crucial for the successful outcome of the entrepreneurial process. If there is a disturbance to this flow of finances, the process may get slowed down, which is followed by a slowing down of the economy. These disturbances can also be due to regional disparities and nonmarket elements. Hence, there is a need to study financial flows to entrepreneurial ventures at every stage of their evolution.

1.1 The Book

This book studies the role of the individual, the region, and nonmarket economics in the interaction between finance and innovation. It is a compendium of papers that address this common motive but stand out as individual papers with a unique message. Four basic units of analysis are considered for these papers: the innovator, the inventor, the region, and groups of countries.

The Innovator: Most of the research that deals with Schumpeter's work concentrates mainly on the characterization of innovation processes (O'Sullivan, 2006); diffusion issue and the topic of allocation of financial resources were more or less neglected. O'Sullivan (2006, p.245) emphasizes, "like Schumpeter, economists of innovation must develop an explicit analysis of ... characteristics for the allocation of resources and, in particular, financial resources." One influential study was by Hall (2002) that initiated this dialogue by asking how research and development expenditure is financed. Two findings stand out clearly: small and new innovative firms face high costs of capital and that there is a strong preference for internal finance. Hall suggests that one needs to study the financing process at the seed level of start-ups in order to understand the dynamics of finance and innovation. Such a study is warranted as financial constraints are much greater for early stage start-ups and the nascent entrepreneurs, who often tend to be more innovative. While the main issue in current research is how to obtain finances for innovation, innovation itself might serve as a useful tool for obtaining external finances. Therefore, the first question that this book addresses is:

- Does innovation help raise external finance at early stages of the start-up process?

The Inventor: The Schumpeterian entrepreneur brings the inventions to market with a motive of profit. In the last five decades, most of the inventions that have reached the market originated in universities (Mowery & Ziedonis, 2002; Mowery, 2006). Commercialization of science took a center stage at many of the universities in the US after the 1980s. Strengthening of patent laws also provided incentives to scientists to commercialize their research. A typical US university technology transfer office informs its scientists: "when an investigator first recognizes that he/she is developing a technology that may have commercial potential he/she should call (disclose it) the Technology Transfer Office."[2] In this manner, the scientist brings the invention to the market. So, do the scientists share the same ambition as the schumpeterian entrepreneur, which is profit? While the process of patenting and invention disclosure may give immense monetary benefits, the motivations of scientists may be different. The second question that this book addresses is:

• Are inventors motivated by prospect of earning money?

The Region: As the start-up grows from seed-stage to being a small firm, it faces further financial constraints (Beck et al., 2005). Flow of credit, as Schumpeter views, is crucial for such firms as that will ensure further investments in the firm. In a perfect market situation money flows to a firm, no matter where it is located. But as financial markets are not perfect, these flows are geographically dispersed. The reasons vary from information asymmetries to operational presence (Patti & Gobbi, 2001) of the lending institution. Especially in a centralized financial system, getting credit is heavily dependent on branch availability within a geographic region (Klagge & Martin, 2005). In this situation, one might argue that allocation of financial resources, debt in particular, is dependent on the type of lending institutions in a particular location. The proximity of informed lenders might encourage small firms to increase their usage of external finance. Therefore, the third question that this book addresses is:

• Once the firm has started, how does the regional financial system affect its finances?

The Unseen Factors: The United Nations emphasizes building technological capability as one way to stimulate economic growth in developing economies (UNDP, 2001). Can the Schumpeterian notion of innovative entrepreneurship, academic entrepreneurship, and efficient systems ensure such development? In addressing this issue, one must recognize the role of nonmarket elements that play a huge role in these economies. One such element is corruption. Not only it is a financial leakage but it is also a "grease" for the bureaucracy to speed-up the regulatory processes for the firm (Leff, 1964). The effect of corruption depends on the level of efficiency in the economy (Méon & Sekkat, 2005). In highly efficient economies with proper judiciary systems, it certainly is a minor element for a single firm, but it is not the case in inefficient economies such as in Africa. It is not yet clear yet if nonmarket elements disturb the Schumpeterian process in such economies. To understand this, one must study how innovative activities are affected by bureaucratic corruption. Hence, the fourth question that this book addresses is:

• Do nonmarket factors play a role in innovation process when it comes to developing economies?

The following section presents a detailed overview of all the four book essays. This is followed by a section on the contributions of the studies and prospects for future research.

1.2   Overview of the Book Essays

1.2.1   Financial Signaling By Innovative Nascent Entrepreneurs

Recently, the relevance of patents for access to external financial resources has been analyzed by Engel and Keilbach (2007), who found that those firms with a higher number of patent applications (size corrected) have a higher probability of obtaining venture capital. Previous studies in the same manner have been restricted to analyzing how existing, incumbent firms are subject to financing constraints. In this study, the focus is on nascent entrepreneurs as financing constraints have the greatest impact on deterring potential entrepreneurs from even starting a new firm.

How can external finance be obtained? Financial signaling theory has suggested that profits and assets can be used as signals to gain finance. But nascent entrepreneurs do not yet earn profits or have very less assets. What they often possess is innovative ideas and intellectual property rights like patents. From a law perspective, patents can serve as signals. Long (2002) shows that patents serve as a signal and patentees use patents for acquiring future benefits rather than only excluding others from accessing their intellectual property (I.P). Patents are primarily information transfer mechanisms (Horstmann et al., 1985) because they convey information about both the invention and the firm. In this manner, appropriability signals potential investors to anticipate the true value of an innovation. Therefore, the signal through patent acts in the mode of *information* and *characteristic* about the firm.

If patents are used to convey information to uninformed potential investors, then at the same time valuable information is also being leaked out to competitors. Bhattacharya and Ritter (1983) call this the "feedback effect equilibrium" for which they suggest using partial disclosure or strategic disclosure as a remedy. There are mainly two reasons why informed agents always find alternatives to safeguard their secrets (while informing potential investors). First, the learning effect, where agents learn about leakage problems and try to find alternatives. The second reason is that when informed agents realize that the same kind of signal is being used by many, they search for other, more unique signals that they can send to stand out. Therefore, when such "signal search" happens, we can assume that always new signals are emerging in the process.

While appropriability indicates the *characteristics* and *information* about the agent, feasibility of the project particularly acts as a signal for the *ability* of the agent. One indicator of feasibility is the development of a prototype. Prototyping is a crucial step in the commercialization process. Prototyping increases the scope and scale of appropriability by enabling the agent to benefit from subsequent intellectual property rights, such as design rights (on the prototype and production designs), copyrights and trademarks, etc. Therefore, the expected benefit from investing in a start-up having prototypes tends to be high for investors, thus increasing the probability of the agent to obtain external finance. Feasibility via prototyping can also signal higher ability and therefore a higher likelihood of obtaining external funding, mainly from investors who want to be part of the start-up and be involved at every stage. This tends to be most relevant in the case of nascent entrepreneurs confronting the most severe credit rationing, as well as information asymmetry problems. A nascent entrepreneur who can signal both appropriability and feasibility therefore has an advantage in terms of obtaining external finance.

We portray our arguments using a simple signaling model to show that having both patents and prototypes sends a stronger signal to investors than having only patents or prototypes. We build a dataset from the USA, called the Innovative Nascent Entrepreneurs Database (INED); a novel dataset where we identify over 900 individuals who are in the process of starting a new business or have just started, along with their financing information. Another novelty in this database is that unlike other existing databases, it provides us with information on development of prototypes and patent ownership. Although we are unable to track these individuals, our dataset allows us to distinguish between nascent entrepreneurs who are planning to start a business and those in the very early start-up stage. After estimating our equations using multinomial methods and several robustness checks, we find that the empirical results support our arguments. The results suggest that nascent entrepreneurs who possess patents as well as prototypes have a higher probability of obtaining equity finance from business angels and venture capitalists. However, we find that the signal matters to investors only if the nascent entrepreneurs are in the early stage of the start-up rather than in the planning stage. Bank finance, however, does not seem to value any of the signals and is based only on collateral.

1.2.2 What Do Scientists Want: Money or Fame?

While the first paper tries to understand how commercialization of innovative activity is coupled with feasibility methods in order to obtain finance, this paper is concerned with motivations of scientists who patent and disclose their inventions. While many studies focus on why firms patent (e.g., Horstmann et al., 1985), very few studies concentrate on why do *individuals* patent. Therefore, this research aims to focus on three factors of interest; namely scientists' internal factors (e.g., human and scientific capital), external factors (directors – research group leader behavior, spin-offs at the institute), and psychological factors (perceptions and motivations).

Etzkowitz (1998) and Slaughter and Leslie (1997) underlined financial rewards, monetary compensation, and profit motive in their analyzes of the new entrepreneurial scientist. Universities that provide greater rewards for scientists' involvement in patenting (e.g., in the forms of equity shares, royalty distribution) are found to motivate scientists to commercialize (patent) more. While the monetary gains from patents are important, an equally intriguing gain is reputation. As individuals are the focus of this study, reputation seems to be another interest that would drive them to act on different things. To be reputable, in the first place, information has to be conveyed about the person in context. In this view, a scientist can be thought of conveying her "type" (highly productive – low productive) to specifically two or more groups of people. One major group would be the colleagues in the research while another can be the employer. To the first group, scientists have three ways to convey information about their type – either publish, or patent, or do both. To the second group, one specific channel would be to report their findings officially. That is, to disclose their invention to the employer on an official basis.

This paper focuses on the channels of patenting and invention disclosure. Both of these can be viewed as information transfer mechanisms not necessarily for monetary gains but for the nonmonetary benefits (Long, 2002) – in this case, reputation – that the individual foresees to be accrued. In a recent study, Jeon and Menicucci (2008) discussed the allocation of talent (brain drain) between the science and private sectors when agents value money and fame. They assumed not only monetary rewards matter in agents decisions but fame, which is defined as peer recognition, matters as well. Individuals therefore would resort to signaling their type by conveying the right information to the concerned group.

For this purpose a unique database was used, which was developed recently at the Max Planck Institute of Economics. This database covers the commercialization activities of over 2,500 scientists spanning over 60 different institutes constituting the Max Planck Society for Advancement of Sciences. Using discrete choice models on patenting and invention disclosure to the MPG, we find that it is not money that influences these decisions, rather it is reputation/fame that drives scientists to both patent and disclose their inventions. Scientists' commercialization activities do not necessarily respond to monetary expectations. This confirms the assertions made by Long (2002) that patenting is basically an information transfer mechanism and patentees use patents not always for the expected financial benefits by excluding others but for the nonmonetary benefits that accrue due to the information conveyed. Therefore, patenting activities could to a certain extent be independent from private economic incentives.

1.2.3 Regional Financial System and Financial Structure of Small Firms

The problem of financial constraints seems to extend beyond the problem of appropriability or innovation. This third study tries to find the factors beyond the firm's purview that may affect firm's financial choices. It extends the study of capital structure of firms to accommodate regional financial characteristics that are generally discussed in the banking literature. Until recently, the two research streams dealing with financing of firms, access to finance and capital structure, have been distinct from each other. Faulkender and Petersen (2006) unite these two in an effort to show that supply of capital is as important as demand for capital in determining capital structure choice of firms. It is still an open issue whether this result is applicable to small firms. This study addresses this issue by empirically testing the effect of regional presence of lending institutions on different financing options and their combinations utilized by small and medium sized firms (SME).

While failure of many small firms can be attributed to the lack of credit availability, composition of firm's finances also plays a crucial role. The small firm capital structure research focuses on this point. Small firms need not respond to market assessments (Chaganti et al., 1995) and therefore could choose to finance themselves with the sources they deem to find useful or obtainable. Also, Romano et al. (2001) rightly note that the dynamic interplay between business characteristics and behavioral characteristics is important in financing decisions.

Earlier work on financial structure concentrated mainly on owner, firm, and industry characteristics in the premise of information asymmetries, agency costs, and signaling. Only recently the concentration has shifted to the specific sources of capital. Faulkender and Petersen (2006, p.46) add that "the same type of market frictions that make capital structure relevant (information asymmetry and investment distortions) also imply that firms sometimes are rationed by their lenders." This indicates at the financial constraints the firm's face and "thus, when estimating a firm's leverage it is important to include not only the determinants of its preferred leverage (the demand side) but also the variables that measure the constraints on a firm's ability to increase its leverage (the supply side)."

While the demand factors may say that small firms resist equity and use mainly internal finance or combine with other financing choices, the supply factors such as availability of financial institutions in the region may in the first place determine the composition of capital structure. If the quantity channel on the regional level is working, then firms will tend to combine more sources of finance that are debt-based or utilize the services of a lending institution – *ceteris paribus*. The same effect may be possible from the price channel (through interest rates etc). Considering small firms, the financial structure takes a wider form including bootstrap financing (asset based lending, factoring, leasing). Most of these are lending technologies and need a presence of a lending institution. Hence, firms may tend to combine these with internal finance if the quantity or price channels are not in operation.

This study empirically tests for the effect of regional presence of lending institutions on different financing options utilized by SMEs. To do so this paper introduces a modified measure of lending operational distance – "commercial operational distance." This measure is calculated for both local as well as national lending institutions. Overall, the analysis is performed for two levels: rural and urban. The central question is how regional commercial operational distance affects the usage and combination of financing sources with traditional sources of finance.

Compiling together a dataset of almost 2,000 SMEs in England with regional lending institution data, the results show that the presence of very local lending institutions affects the likelihood of urban small firms to combine retained earnings with only debt or debt and boot strap or debt, bootstrap and equity. These combinations are not utilized by small firms that are in the regions where banks and semi-local lending institutions exist. They would rather depend on internal financing. For rural small firms, the presence of lending institutions does not matter. In fact, high presence of any lending institution does not change the preference for internal finance. Also, the effect of quantity channel when all lending institutions are present in a region was tested. High combined presence also does not deter small firms from using internal finance both in rural and urban areas. The two reasons for these are that small firms may rely on internal finance as the quantity and price channels of lending institutions do not seem to work and if they do work its only for very local lending institutions. The second reason might be that due to riskier firms approaching for debt, monitoring costs are pushed on to the borrower or credit rationing might trigger usage of internal finance only. In the case of small firms, Faulkender and Petersen (2006)'s proposition that usage of debt will increase with increase in suppliers of capital stands true only with respect to increase in very local suppliers of finance and not with all.

1.2.4 Corruption and Innovation: A Grease or Sand Relationship?

Most of the developing economies face the problem of inherent inefficiencies in economic, political, and legal systems. In such inefficient environments, it is questionable if undertaking innovative activity is free of any nonmarket effects. Financial leakages like bureaucratic corruption are assumed to affect innovative activity adversely, but never a proper study was undertaken to validate this assumption. Interestingly, Leff (1964) also claims that bureaucratic corruption helps to speed-up processes and help economic growth. Also, before a claim is made that innovation helps raise finance, one needs to also consider financial leakages that hinder or may encourage innovative activity in inefficient economies. The step to link innovation to corruption is important because, on the one hand, the innovation research scarcely considers nonmarket factors and, on the other hand, public choice literature scarcely considers the role of innovation.

Considering the possible adverse effects of corruption, the following arguments are put forward in this study. First, innovative firms need faster approvals of permits, new licenses, and permissions to get new technology as fast as possible. If these have to come through a heavily bureaucratic structure, the time lag involved would ultimately cost the firms a market lead advantage. Second, if the financial markets were thought of as perfect, any loss to investment due to corruption costs could have been made up for. On the investment angle therefore, corruption can be seen as hindering R&D investment or early stage investments mainly in the presence of imperfect financial markets. Third, in centralized economies parallel projects involving high uncertainties are discouraged by bureaucracy. This is especially true if projects are government funded rather than private funded. In such cases, the firm's optimal R&D is either not reached or never undertaken, making the firm stick to routinized activities in the industry it belongs to. Hence corruption can sand the wheels of innovation.

On the other hand, corruption has a beneficial feature too, especially in inefficient economies. If the officials allot permits to the firm that has a higher ability to bribe, then it wins the innovation race and therefore a market lead. When firms undertake or wish to invest in incremental innovation, corruption can act as a regular feature that a firm has to undertake to avoid any uncertainty. The third dimension is jumping the policy hurdle. Leff (1964) and Bailey (1966) view corruption as a reaction to bad policies and hence helps jump the policy hurdle.

Which kind of innovative activity does corruption affect in what way? A firm can be having more than one kind of innovative activity and not all of them might be affected by corruption at all! Considering bureaucratic corruption, activities that require exclusive involvement of government (permissions, etc.) might be affected and not necessarily the others. For streamlining the argument, the "grease the wheels" vs. "sand the wheels" hypothesis is tested on the four types of innovation – product, process, marketing, and organizational innovation. To test the grease/sand effect, countries in the African continent are considered where governance structures are often considered to be weak and therefore become a right set of countries to use.

This study tries to contribute to the literature on innovation and public choice by exploring this issue by using a large-scale firm-level database – the World Bank Enterprise Survey conducted in 2004.[3] Using probit and instrumental variable probit models, the results show that corruption (as a percentage of sales revenue) hinders product innovation and organizational innovation and has a positive effect on marketing innovation. Process innovation, however, does not get affected. Hence in inefficient economies, while giving any policy advice on innovation, one needs to account for nonmarket factors such as corruption.

1.3 Contributions and Future Directions of Research

This book improves our understanding of how finance, innovation, and corruption interact with each other. Specifically, how innovation is utilized as a "signal" to gain monetary and nonmonetary benefits and how regional supply of finance also affects financial structure of small firms. Given these points, we also learn that nonmarket factors affect innovation. Given that the World is back to yet another serious financial crisis, the implications of the book are important. The rising financial constraints would lead to investors demanding more signals to assure of the quality of investment. Scientists therefore have an opportunity if they wish to start-up, in that they have the desired signals of patent and prototypes. Firms are going to look for financial resources more locally; therefore, local community banking and cooperative banking may find themselves again in higher demand. Developing countries that have to deal with decrease in foreign direct investments and resource crunch first need to clear the black-economy that is hindering innovation. Even though corruption is sometimes good for marketing innovation, it does not mean that the firms desire it always. If the systems are made efficient, then innovative activity shall rise in developing economies. This would help them to face at least some economic risks in future.

A main contribution of this book is that it tries to combine different fields for each of the four studies. While the first paper combines economics of innovation and finance, the second combines commercialization of science with individual oriented research focusing on motivations. In a similar vein, the third paper extends the field of geography of finance to focus on firms and combine it with banking and small firm finance literature. The fourth paper combined the fields of economics of innovation with public choice theory, specially focusing on nonmarket elements. All the four studies have each a new insight that can be advanced further.

Future Directions: To evaluate the future potential of the general ideas presented in this book, two steps are crucial: short-run goals and long-run goals. The short-run goals are very specific to each of the papers in this book and I discuss these goals first. This is followed by the long-run orientation of the entire theme of this book.

Signaling theory also indicates learning about signals and how to evaluate them. The next task to extend this would be to create a learning-based model on how entrepreneurs as well as financiers learn from each other. Data on project-wise financing and collect elicitation of entrepreneurs and financiers on what they consider as true signals would be a more direct test for this purpose. Entrepreneurs tend to always find new ways to finance themselves, so there is always a continuous learning in financing their projects. Another way to extend Chap. 3 is to find if entrepreneurs too value reputation. Entrepreneurship also leads to changes in group status, so does that mean that reputation also plays a role? The future focus of the regional financial system project is to concentrate on completely measuring different dimensions of the system and relating it to regional economic activity. If regional innovation systems are helpful, one cannot but agree that the regional financial system also plays a role in sustaining that development. Finally, if one has to give policy related advice to developing economies on innovation and financing, it is very important to understand the effect of non-market components. Apart from bureaucratic corruption, there are other types of corruption such a political and informal corruption. The extension of the corruption paper lies in exploring the effect of these types on innovation. Not only types of innovation, but different types of corruption are also important in deciding economic outcomes. The goal therefore would be to analyze the link between corruption and economic growth via innovation.

Thinking broadly, it is very important to understand entrepreneurship, innovation, and finance in terms of all units of analysis. As this book has shown, it is useful to look at the inventor, innovator, regional, and nonmarket perspectives. It is especially important in current times, when, on the one hand, dynamic start-ups are aiming to become successful up-starts; on the other hand, the financial environment threatens this optimism with its uncertainies.

To gain meaningful answers to economic questions as these, one has to reframe the questions themselves. As this book has shown, it is also good to ask if innovation itself can raise finances than viewing this relation the other way round. It is useful to consider the entrepreneurial edge issue if one goes back to Schumpeter and asks if this "edge" also paves way through difficult times as a financial crisis. As an economic problem, one can view it as the comparative advantage of innovation in raising finances, not just in static terms but by actually extending it to dynamic analyzes.

In a situation where a scientist takes the invention to the market and becomes an entrepreneur, one can understand that the motivation might be money. What economic research is still to identify is whether these "scientist entrepreneurs" manage finances in their start-ups differently than others and whether financing is at all a problem for them. If not, then the system as such has been successful in generating healthy firms.

As mentioned earlier, this entrepreneurial edge has an optimistic side as well as a pessimistic side to it. Even when the firm displays immense potential, it is not guaranteed that it will be a smooth ride. The role of institutions matters most in determining a life-span of any firm. There is a need to understand much further if formal and informal institutions, especially that are related to finance, shape the motivations of entrepreneurs or are hurdles to entrepreneurship. At least in developing economies the impact of informal side of institutions on level of entrepreneurial activity is quite large. If the lessons from developed countries have to be applied to developing countries, one cannot forget including the nonmarket factors. Be it the economic analyzes of innovation-led growth or green-technologies, it is always better to include nonmarket factors. Only then, we can come up with "customized solutions" to economic problems of different countries.

The entrepreneurial edge is important. It is important not just for overall economic growth but also for individual development. The main reason why many countries differ in this edge is due to differences in business and cultural environment. In the 1980s Japan was most innovative, but now it finds itself in recession. At the same time, countries like Germany continuously produce inventions and bring them to the market, but culturally, failure is treated as bad for the individual, unlike in the United States. In developing countries like India, working as a salaried person is treated as a much secure option than working as a self-employed person. So, looking at these examples, one can say that this entrepreneurial edge affects economic growth in different countries, depending on the socio-economic-political context. To achieve this, a scientific approach would involve a multidisciplinary effort to track role of motivations, learning, and hurdles to entrepreneurial edge as a key for economic growth.

Notes

[1] John Wright, Chairman of the Federation of Small Businesses in the UK in an open letter in October 2008 to Chancellor of the Exchequer Alistair Darling. Source: www.fsb.org.uk

[2] source: http://techtransfer.byu.edu/Resources/. Similar statements can be found on TTO websites of different universities.

[3] Enterprise Surveys, The World Bank Group. http://www.enterprisesurveys.org/

Chapter 2
Financial Signaling by Innovative Nascent Entrepreneurs

INNOVATIVE NEW VENTURES fail if they cannot attract resources needed to commercialize new ideas and inventions. Obtaining external resources is a central issue for *nascent entrepreneurs* – people who are in the process of starting new ventures. They rarely have sufficient internal resources to finance their startup activities. One important problem is of information asymmetries between nascent entrepreneurs and external financiers. Although the US venture capital industry has grown dramatically in the past 30 years, information asymmetries may still inhibit the commercialization of innovative ideas. In fact, as Hsu (2004, p.1805) puts it, "particularly for entrepreneurs without an established reputation, convincing external resource providers such as venture capitalists (VCs) to provide financial capital may be challenging."

Information asymmetries are likely to be a severe problem, especially for innovative new ventures in the *earliest stage* of the startup process. Innovative nascent entrepreneurs developing their business concepts and operating businesses that do not yet generate revenues tend to possess assets that are knowledge-based and intangible. Consequently, the quality and value of the new venture cannot be directly observed.

Recently, the relevance of patents for access to external financial resources has been analyzed by Engel and Keilbach (2007). Using a dataset consisting of young German firms, they found that those firms with a higher number of patent applications (size corrected) have a higher probability of obtaining venture capital. This result is in line with the findings reported by Hellman and Puri (2000). Their results suggest that innovators are more likely to obtain venture capital financing than are imitators.

However, patents provide only one signal. Gompers and Lerner (2001, p.35), for instance, warn that "Although more tangible than an idea, patents and trademarks themselves are not enough to enable a company to obtain financing from most lenders. A soft asset such as patent may have value only when it is combined with other assets, such as the entrepreneur's knowledge of a particular process or technology that the patent involves." In this paper, we argue that innovative nascent entrepreneurs can cope with the problem of asymmetric information by

P. Mahagaonkar, *Money and Ideas: Four Studies on Finance, Innovation and the Business Life Cycle*, International Studies in Entrepreneurship 25, DOI 10.1007/978-1-4419-1228-2_2, © Springer Science+Business Media, LLC 2010

using patents and prototypes in order to signal the commercial potential of their innovative ideas to potential investors. While patents are a means to protect property rights and signal the entrepreneur's ability to appropriate the returns of an innovation (*appropriability*), prototypes signal the actual *feasibility* of the proposed project. For people who are in the process of starting a business or have just started, prototypes may be the crucial link that actually provides additional value to patents as signals and thus make financing easier.

Moreover, previous studies have been restricted to analyzing how existing, incumbent firms are subject to financing constraints. Yet, it may be that financing constraints have the greatest impact on deterring potential entrepreneurs from even starting a new firm. Cassar (2004, p.279) states that for analysis of the financing of business start-ups "the ideal sample would consist of entrepreneurs in the process of starting a venture and tracking these entrepreneurs through the initial stages of business formation." In this paper, we therefore shift the lens away from established, incumbent firms, to nascent entrepreneurs. We use a new dataset to address the point emphasized by Cassar (2004). Our sample consists of 906 individuals who are in the *process* of starting a new venture. Although we are unable to track these individuals, our dataset allows us to distinguish between nascent entrepreneurs who are planning to start a business and those in the very early start-up stage. In contrast to existing empirical studies, our paper eliminates the problem of *survivorship bias* in the sample because we analyze ventures at birth. Moreover, our sample enables us to identify if entrepreneurs possess patents and prototypes along with information on external sources of finance.

Hence, we contribute to the existing empirical literature on external finance of innovative new ventures by investigating the relevance of patents and prototype for the external finance of innovative nascent entrepreneurs.[1]

We portray our arguments using a simple signaling model to show that having both patents and prototypes sends a stronger signal to investors than having only patents or prototypes. The empirical results support our arguments. The results suggest that nascent entrepreneurs who possess patents as well as prototypes have a higher probability of obtaining equity finance from business angels and venture capitalists. However, we find that the signal matters to investors only if the nascent entrepreneurs are in the early stage of the startup rather than the planning stage. Bank finance, however, does not seem to value any of the signals and is based only on collateral.

In the following section we discuss the issue of financial constraints for innovative firms, followed by a detailed discussion of appropriablity and feasibility issues and their relation to financing constraints. We then use a similar signaling model as of M. Spence (1973) to develop our hypotheses. Section 2.3 introduces the data used and provides some descriptive statistics; Sect. 2.4 presents empirical results and Sect. 2.5 concludes.

2.1 Literature and Hypothesis Development

2.1.1 *Financial Constraints of Innovative Nascent Entrepreneurs*

Why are innovative nascent entrepreneurs financially constrained? This involves three main factors. The first factor is information asymmetries, which arise if the firm has better information about the returns occurring from their investment in intangible assets than do potential investors. Hence, "external finance may be expensive, if available at all, because of adverse selection and moral hazard problems" (Carpenter & Petersen, 2002, p.F56). It is likely that information asymmetries are higher for nascent entrepreneurs who do not have any established track record.

The second factor involves the fundamental uncertainty inherent in knowledge and new ideas. As Arrow (1962) pointed out, this uncertainty characterizes the relationship between innovative efforts, or inputs into the innovation process, and their resulting outcomes. New knowledge is intrinsically uncertain in its potential economic value (Arrow, 1962). Thus, "the challenge to decision making is ignorance, the fact that nobody really knows anything" (O'Sullivan, 2006, p.257), or at least, anything for sure. So the degree of uncertainty inherent in the innovative process renders the decisions by potential investors to be based on subjective judgments, which may or may not coincide with the assessment by the nascent entrepreneur. This implies that innovative activity may be burdened with difficulties in obtaining finance, even at the prevailing market interest rates. While this problem exists for all firms per se, one can argue that in the case of nascent entrepreneurs, potential investors tread their path extra carefully and many times abstain from investing in the seed stage itself. Moreover, nascent entrepreneurs, due to inexperience, may not qualify for finance through the subjective judgments/heuristics commonly used by the investors.

The third factor, also pointed out by Arrow (1962), involves the propensity for knowledge to exhibit, at least partly, characteristics and properties of a public good, that is, it is nonexcludable and nonrival in use. Thus, to fully appropriate investments in innovative activity, the associated intellectual property must be protected through some regime such as patents, copyrights, or secrecy. If knowledge spills over to other firms, the benefits accruing from innovation cannot be fully appropriated by the innovating firm.

Taken together, uncertainty, knowledge asymmetries, and the potential nonexclusive nature of investments in intangible assets make it difficult to evaluate the expected value of an innovative firm, especially of an innovative nascent firm (Audretsch & Weigand, 2005).

While problems with innovation are universal, one may therefore ask the question, "why consider nascent entrepreneurs?" In recent years, a number of empirical studies have investigated external financing of innovative firms. However, most of these studies have been based on financing innovative activity in incumbent firms that already exist (Hall, 2002). While existing firms have at least some history, nascent entrepreneurs are people who have not even founded a new firm, and in some sense can be placed to the left of zero of the firm-age distribution and at zero for the firm size distribution. These conditions that are strongly associated with nascent entrepreneurship should exceed those for a new venture that is actually launched and a startup subsequently matures over its life cycle. Thus, nascent entrepreneurs would be expected to face financing constraints at least as great, but presumably even greater, than do new ventures.

2.1.2 How Can Nascent Entrepreneurs Overcome Financial Constraints?

One might argue that if appropriability of innovation can be ensured, it may help nascent entrepreneurs to overcome the financing problems. While this may be true, one cannot ignore the problem with the present systems of appropriability – namely patent, trademarks, etc. While, on the one hand, some degree of appropriability is being ensured, on the other, hand valuable information is leaked in the process to unrelated parties, mostly competitors. Apart from this, the three previously mentioned problems with innovation still have to be addressed. Our aim in this paper is therefore to show that "feasibility" serves as a useful signal on this aspect too. To do so we first deal with the present markets for knowledge and then discuss the usefulness of appropriability as a signal. We then suggest the reasons why feasibility is needed as a reinforcing mechanism to appropriability.

Let us consider the problem of knowledge as a public good. The markets for knowledge create opportunities for increasing investment in innovation. From the policy perspective, the intellectual property system is encouraged mainly to ensure the appropriability of innovation and induce increases in investment further. Intellectual property(I.P) rights are the result of government intervention through which appropriability can be ensured from research and development and further investments can be encouraged (in the line of thought followed by Arrow (1962), Nelson (1959), and R. C. Levin et al. (1987)). As the European Commission[2] explains, "One direct means (to stop leakage of knowledge) is the strengthening of the appropriability conditions through an effective system of intellectual property rights." Entrepreneurs have to resort to private financing although public support is also in some cases. Most of the nascent entrepreneurs self-finance innovative activities and try to deploy protection mechanisms that per se ensure appropriability. The question remains as to whether appropriability mechanisms such as patents can serve as a reliable signal to external investors to obtain more investment.

Can patents serve as signals? From a law perspective, they do. Long (2002) shows that patents serve as a signal and patentees use patents for acquiring future benefits rather than only excluding others from accessing their intellectual property. The several reasons why patents can be used as signals are summarized by Long (2002). Patents are primarily information transfer mechanisms (Horstmann et al., 1985). In this manner they convey information about both the invention and the firm. In general, market actors believe patents are correlated with various desirable firm attributes.

Anton and Yao (2004) suggest that whether an innovation becomes patented depends on the amount of the information to be disclosed to the intellectual property markets leading to "little patents and big secrets." In this manner appropriability (by way of I.P) signals potential investors to anticipate the true value of an innovation.

While we address the problem of public good, patents seem to somehow be utilized as a channel through which the information asymmetry problem can also be addressed. The signal through patent acts in the mode of *information* and *characteristic* about the firm. Development of an invention from an idea and a concept to a patent indicates that the firm has prospective competent characteristics required in the market. The benefit to the investor when the firm fails to commercialize successfully generally includes rights and conditions that may sometimes also share royalties accruing from the patent along with other intellectual property monetary benefits. In this way investments in start-ups by entrepreneurs holding I.P and ion particular patents may be considered partly secured, provided contracts are properly drawn. This view has been quite prevalent with venture capital and private equity investments.

Increasingly, patent protection has been the main factor for VCs in making the decision of whether or not to invest (Hayes, 1999). As in the job market models, potential candidates observe the characteristic (degrees) potential employers value and try to obtain them beforehand to signal their productivity. Nascent entrepreneurs could also be considered to be attracted to patenting in order to signal commercializability of their ideas.[3] On the other hand, "Venture capitalists use client patents (or more likely, patent applications) as evidence that the company is well managed, is at a certain stage in development, and has defined and carved out a market niche"(Lemley, 2001, p.14).

If patenting seems to be a good signal, a crucial element still remains. If patents are actually used to convey information to uninformed potential investors, then at the same time valuable information is also being leaked out to competitors. Bhattacharya and Ritter (1983) call this the "feedback effect equilibrium." Anton and Yao (2002) take a similar view. Both these papers then suggest either partial disclosure or strategic disclosure as a remedy. These models inherently assume that the firm is confronted with only one way of information disclosure and that is not without leakage problems. It would be therefore worthwhile to have a deeper look at this assumption. There are mainly two reasons why informed agents always find alternatives to safeguard their secrets (while informing potential investors). First, the learning effect, where agents learn about leakage problems and try to find alternatives. The second reason is that when informed agents realize that the same kind of signal is being used by many, they search for other, more unique signals that they can send to stand out. Therefore, when such "signal search" happens, we can assume that in the process always new signals are emerging. In what follows we show that patenting is accompanied by a different signal for the informed agent to benefit from signaling.

How to address the problem of fundamental uncertainty? While appropriability indicates the *characteristics* and *information* about the agent, feasibility of the project particularly acts as a signal for the *ability* of the agent. One indicator of feasibility is the development of a prototype. What is ability in the eyes of an investor? Broadly we can think of manufacturing ability: ability to ensure a sound pricing and costing strategy. This would mean a big step ahead of the business plan. Every principal seeks to find such agents that would signal future plans and profitability as accurately as possible. Even though advanced planning techniques exist to provide accurate numeric forecasts, the ability of a prototype to signal success or failure of the start-up is even higher. Mitigating information asymmetries and the quality of a signal remains a crucial step in reducing financing constraints. A stronger signal that can substantially reduce information asymmetry is the development of a prototype.

Prototyping is a crucial step in the commercialization process. In some cases prototyping makes patenting easier, and in some cases it serves as a crucial link to the patent and final realization of the finished marketable product. When an agent possesses a prototype, she/he can clearly determine the processes required for large-scale production, the resources needed and the best suppliers can be charted out. Hence production plans can be strengthened. Once the production plans are clearly defined, the costs and the pricing strategy can be accurately approximated by the agent. Business plan projections become much accurate, and therefore having a prototype serves as a signal to decrease information asymmetry (it also reduces the uncertainty inherent in the project).

Prototyping also increases the scope and scale of appropriability by enabling the agent to benefit from subsequent intellectual property rights, such as design rights (on the prototype and production designs), copyrights and trademarks etc. Therefore, the expected benefit from investing in a start-up having prototypes tends to be high for investors, thus increasing the probability of the agent to obtain external finance. An interesting experiment at the Cranfield Institute of Technology (Hilal & Soltan, 1992) found the following advantages with the prototyping approach as compared to the non prototyping (structured development approach).

1. The prototyping approach was found to be more robust to sudden and major changes (such as absence of an expert due to illness).
2. It provides a "superior environment for knowledge elicitation, where a domain expert is available, through the mechanism of allowing the expert to criticize working models of the final system."
3. Prototyping approach allows for greater flexibility in project planning.
4. "Testing" can be done throughout the project, while in the non-prototyping approach it is left until the very end.

Feasibility via prototyping can also signal higher ability and therefore a higher likelihood of obtaining external funding, mainly from investors who want to be part of the start-up process and be involved at every stage. This tends to be most relevant in the case of nascent entrepreneurs confronting the most severe credit rationing, as well as information asymmetry problems. A nascent entrepreneur who can signal both appropriability and feasibility therefore has an advantage in terms of obtaining external finance. In this way the problems of information asymmetry, fundamental uncertainty, and public good nature of knowledge can be significantly decreased.

This feature may not be as straightforward as it seems and may be affected by the sector (in some sectors patenting is not the first priority) and risk taking attitude of the investor, even though the signals are strong and reduce the extent of information asymmetries. Such a case would happen mainly when the entrepreneur serves as the link between the idea and an actual start-up.

2.1.3 Appropriability and Feasibility as Signals to Investors

In this section we adopt a simple M. A. Spence (1973)- type model to portray our arguments that appropriability and feasibility can serve as signals and present our hypotheses. We assume that informed agents are trying to signal uninformed agents about the commercializability of their innovative ideas. What is inherent is their commercializability types of ideas can be distinguished in the following manner. *Types*: Commercializable ideas are denoted by type-high-h, and non commercializable ideas as type-low-l.

The Basic Model

The game first begins by nature determining the type of idea. Investors hold a common prior, μ_0. This is the probability of the type being type-h and reflects the prior belief of investors regarding the fraction of type-h ideas in the market. Individuals owning the ideas choose to appropriate the benefits of innovation by choosing different appropriability mechanisms (patent, prototype, or both). Investors observe the extent of appropriability (denoted by e) and update their beliefs regarding the type of each idea. Each investor then decides which idea she/he is willing to consider as a potential investment.

Appropriability and feasibility are costly. Legal costs, other direct monetary costs, opportunity costs, etc. have to be borne by the nascent entrepreneurs.[4] These costs are generally high and have to be financed using own money. As is intuitive, these costs increase with the number of appropriability and feasibility mechanisms utilized. The cost of these mechanisms to an extent of effort e for a type-h idea is given by

$$C_h(e) = \frac{1}{2}\theta e^2; \quad 0 < \theta < 1 \tag{2.1}$$

and the cost of type-l is given by $C_l(e) = \frac{1}{2}e^2$.

As different mechanisms are possible and are of different value to the firm, we consider these under a continuum with a ranking such that having a patent and also a prototype is ranked highest against having only a prototype, only a patent, or nothing. It can therefore be observed that costs increase with the rank assigned. Precisely, C increases with an increase in e(also the single crossing and spence-mirrlees condition).

Value of Ideas to Investors: Investors are assumed to be unable to perceive the true value of an idea. Investment in an idea therefore depends on its commercializability. As commercializability itself cannot be perfectly estimated, investors would therefore prefer those ideas that signal strong "credentials," in this case, strong appropriability and feasibility. The value of the idea is therefore assumed to be $v_t(e) = \alpha_t + \beta_t e$, *where*

- $v_h = \alpha_h \geq v_l = \alpha_l$,
- $\partial v_h / \partial e = \beta_h \geq \partial v_l / \partial e = \beta_l, \forall e \geq 0$.

This shows how each investor would value ideas, where t is the type and e is the extent of appropriability and feasibility (A&F). The first point implies that investors attach an intrinsically higher value to a type-h idea and second, valuation of an idea increases linearly with the extent of A&F, with the rate of increase being slightly higher for type-h idea. For purpose of simplicity, we assume $\alpha_l = \beta_l = 0$, which means that the value for a type-l idea is set to zero, by the investor.

Equilibrium Analysis

We will now analyze the equilibrium of this signaling model and will show that the probability of obtaining external finance increases with the strength of the signal.[5]

Complete information: Assume that the type of idea is common knowledge. This means type-h ideas will be believed as type-h with probability one and as type-l with zero probability. The optimal extent of A&F by entrepreneurs would be

$$e_{h \to 1}^* = \operatorname{argmax}_e [v_h(e) - C_h(e)],$$
$$e_{l \to 0}^* = \operatorname{argmax}_e [v_l(e) - C_l(e)],$$
$$\Rightarrow e_{h \to 1}^* = \beta / \theta \text{ and } e_{l \to 0}^* = 0, \text{ with } e_{h \to 1}^* > e_{l \to 0}^*. \qquad (2.2)$$

Thus, the best response of entrepreneurs with type-h ideas would be always to choose higher level of A&F.

Asymmetric Information (AI): In the case of asymmetric information, a separating equilibrium can be derived. Generally two cases of envy and nonenvy need to be defined. Here we discuss only the nonenvy case where the owners of type-l ideas have no incentive to falsely signal their idea being type-h. A separating equilibrium involves the choice of a strictly higher extent of A&F by entrepreneurs having type-h ideas than of type-l ideas. A minimum level of A&F is required so that types of ideas could be differentiated. This minimum level is the maximum level that a type-l idea owner will be able to afford. This is given by

$$\bar{e}_l = \beta + \sqrt{\beta^2 + 2\alpha} = e_h^{\text{AI}}. \qquad (2.3)$$

Therefore, the proposed equilibrium strategies would be $(e_h^{eq}, e_l^{eq}) = (0, \bar{e}_l)$.

The beliefs of investors on equilibrium path would be

$$\mu(h/e) = \begin{cases} 1, & e \geq \bar{e}_l \\ 0, & e < \bar{e}_l. \end{cases} \tag{2.4}$$

This implies that investors consider an idea to be type-h only if the extent of A&F is greater than the minimum level that certainly differentiates the types. Based on the above, the value of ideas to investors can be shown as, $v = \begin{cases} \alpha + \beta e, & e \geq \bar{e}_l \\ 0, & e < \bar{e}_l \end{cases}$.

Clearly the best response of entrepreneurs with type-h ideas to investors' beliefs and strategies would be to choose $\bar{e}_l (e_l^* \rightarrow 0)$.

Based on the above equilibrium analysis, we arrive at the basic hypothesis that the probability of obtaining external finance increases with the strength of the signal (A&F).[6]

To extend the main hypothesis, it is also interesting to consider who may actually finance in this type of signaling scenario. Ueda (2004) puts forward a similar signaling approach to show that it is the entrepreneur with little collateral and tight protection of IPR that drives the entrepreneur to approach the venture capitalist for financing due to decreases in threat of expropriation. These propositions are consistent with our model. The fact that the entrepreneur realizes the value of tight IPR and also the disadvantages of having low collateral is consistent with the insight that the entrepreneurs use IPR to serve as a signal. More recently, Engel and Keilbach (2007) show that "higher innovativeness in venture funded firms is due to the selection process of the venture capitalist prior to the funding rather than to the venture funding itself." Venture capitalists accomplish this by selecting firms that already have patents prior to obtaining funding. Our model though hypothesizes that even if tighter IPR regime and patents are present, in many cases the entrepreneurs with stronger signals (feasibility) may acquire external finance and possibly equity would play a prominent role. In the empirical analysis we not only concentrate on VCs (which are well versed in receiving signals) but also on business angels and show that signals work with them as well.

Other studies that have used the signaling approach: Myers and Majluf (1984), for example, have used a similar signaling game but they assumed the firm to be already earning positive profits. Leland and Pyle (1977) also have used a signaling approach to convey that firms can obtain external finance if they could signal their market value via offering costly collaterals. Similarly, Bhattacharya and Ritter (1983) assume that signaling can occur only through channels that lead to leakage of knowledge. In our approach, we show that signaling can also occur through intangible assets and the firms need not achieve profits beforehand (as they are nascent entrepreneurs). In addition, it can also be observed that having a prototype is probably a reliable way to avoid any leakage of sensitive information about innovations to competitors. To empirically test our hypotheses, we use discrete choice models on a new dataset of nascent entrepreneurs, which is explained in the following section.

2.2   Data

2.2.1   *Building the Innovative Nascent Entrepreneurs Database (INED)*

To test the two main propositions linking the financial structure of nascent entrepreneurs to their ability to undertake and signal innovative activity, the types of data sets providing information about the financial structure of (new) firms that have been used in previous studies are of little use. This is because of the focus in this paper on nascent entrepreneurs rather than established firms, however, young they may be. Thus, a very different type of dataset providing information on both individuals who are considering launching a new venture, that is nascent entrepreneurs, as well as their innovative activity and financial prospects is required to test the hypotheses posited in the previous section.

Finding a dataset possessing information both on nascent entrepreneurs' innovation activity and their finance is rare. In this paper a new data set is developed and applied, which consists of 4,122 entrepreneurs (including individuals who are considering launching a new business), investors, and others. The data set was created for the Ewing Marion Kauffman Foundation by the Center for Innovative Entrepreneurship (CIE) in May–June 2005 and consists of a web-based survey of potential entrepreneurs. CIE surveyed visitors of the web site http://www. vfinance.com, which is a location for entrepreneurs seeking finance and interested in finding the names of potential angel investors or venture capital firms. CIE implemented the survey using two methods. This first was to send each web site visitor an email inviting her to participate in the survey. The second method involved soliciting a random sample of web site visitors to participate in the survey. An important qualification of this database involves selection bias. The database consists solely of individuals sufficiently interested in obtaining finance that they visited the web site. Thus, individuals not interested in obtaining finance for a new venture are not included in the data base. However, it is important to emphasize that the two major hypotheses do not imply starting with a sample of individuals representative of the overall working population and then identifying which ones constitute nascent entrepreneurs. Rather, in this study the starting point should consist of individuals who are already nascent entrepreneurs. Thus, the appropriate database should exclude those not considering launching a new venture and include only those individuals who can be reasonably classified as being a nascent entrepreneur. Thus, while the well-known PSED (Panel Study of Entrepreneurial Dynamics), for instance, is a representative sample of American adults and was initiated to "provide systematic, reliable, and generalizable data on important features of the entrepreneurial or start-up process" (Reynolds et al., 2004), it is more appropriate for testing hypotheses distinguishing between nascent and non-nascent entrepreneurs. While the sampling mechanism used in PSED is appropriate to generate a sample that is nationally representative with respect to population characteristics, like age or education, it might not be ideal to analyze innovative nascent entrepreneurs' sources of external finance, where a database consisting solely of innovative nascent entrepreneurs is more appropriate.

As pointed out by Davidsson (2006, p. 55) the downside of the "representative" sample provided by the PSED "is that the sample will be very heterogeneous and dominated by imitative, low-potential ventures." He therefore suggests to "use other sampling mechanisms than probability sampling in order to get sufficient numbers of high-tech firms, for instance" (Davidsson, 2006, p.56). In this respect, the database used in this paper based on the CIE survey is a valuable source of information about innovative nascent entrepreneurs, who are, by definition, *seeking finance*. Moreover, as the descriptive statistics presented in Sect. 4 show, the share of innovative entrepreneurs included in this database is strikingly high.

2.2.2 Variable Definitions

While the PSED database consists of a sample presumably reflecting characteristics of the overall population, we created the Innovative Nascent Entrepreneurs Database (INED) from the CIE survey to consist solely of nascent entrepreneurs. However, in creating the INED, a similar criteria were used that a respondent had to meet in order to be considered as a nascent entrepreneur. In particular, for an individual to be classified as a nascent entrepreneur in the PSED, each record had to meet three criteria: (1)"now trying to start a new business," (2)"currently active in a startup effort" and "anticipates part or full ownership of the new business," and (3)"has NOT yet attained positive monthly cash flow that covered expenses and the owner–manager salaries for more than 3 months" (Reynolds et al., 2004, p. 268).

For the INED, an individual was similarly classified as being a nascent entrepreneur if the three following analogous conditions were met:

- The individual is seeking capital to start a new business
- The individual intends to be owner or part owner of the business
- The business has not generated revenues in 2004 and 2005

Respondents claiming 0% ownership or having positive revenues in 2004–2005 were not classified as being nascent entrepreneurs. The questions included in the survey are included in the appendix. The sample can be distinguished as consisting of two major groups, or sub-samples – a group of individuals engaged in the planning stage for starting a new firm and the group of individuals actually engaged in the launch of a new venture. An individual was classified as a planning stage nascent entrepreneur, or belonging to the former group, if she/he was (1) planning to start a new business, and (2) the start-up was not a business yet, in that it is not in operation and no products or services have been launched or offered for sale. By contrast, a respondent was classified as being in the early start-up stage if a venture had been launched but was not generating revenue, and if at least a concept had been developed.

Those reporting that they started their business before 2005 and/or that the number of employees, not counting the owners, exceeds one were excluded from the first group (planning stage nascent entrepreneurs). Similarly, those respondents reporting that they started their business before 2003 and/or that the number of employees exceeds ten were excluded from the second group (incipient start-ups). These stringent criteria were for classifying nascent entrepreneurs as either planning stage or incipient start-ups were applied to maintain the integrity and consistency of the data.

External source of finance: The data set contains information about the sources of business financing. Entrepreneurs reported whether they used the following external financing sources to establish their business: (1) bank loans to the business, (2) home equity loan in an owner's name, (3) other bank loans in an owner's name, (4) venture funds in exchange for stock/ownership in company, and (5) individual investors or companies in exchange for stock/ownership in company. While the first three sources are indicators of debt, the last two sources represent indicators of equity. The consistency of the responses was checked and verified. First, those records where respondents reported equity finance and 100% ownership were excluded from the sample. Second, those records where a respondent reported owning 0% of the business and at the same time reported having equity as a source of business financing were also excluded from the sample.

Patents and prototype: In the survey, entrepreneurs were asked the following question, "Does your business own or have you applied for a patent that is essential to the business?" This question was used to compute the dummy variable "patents," which takes the value one if the answer is YES and zero otherwise. Respondents were also asked "Where is your business in the start-up process?" This question was used to compute the dummy variable "prototype" which takes the value one if the answer is "prototype developed" and zero otherwise.

Business relevant information: The data set contains additional information about the entrepreneur and the proposed start-up. In particular, records indicate whether a business plan was written, whether the business has international links, whether the respondent is a serial entrepreneur, whether the business was started by a single person or a team of people, and whether the respondent owns a house that can be used as collateral (see Appendix for the questions asked).

2.2.3 Descriptive Statistics

The means and standard deviations of all variables are reported in Table 2.1. As can be seen from the table, 12% of the nascent entrepreneurs in the planning stage use debt as an external source of finance. By contrast, 19% of nascent incipient entrepreneurs in the very early stage of the venture rely on debt. With respect to equity finance, the difference between both the planning and the incipient entrepreneurs is even larger. While only 6% of nascent entrepreneurs in the planning stage have equity finance, more than 20% of the nascent entrepreneurs in the early start-stage have equity finance. These differences are statistically significant at the 1% level. Nascent entrepreneurs in the planning stage choose either debt (25%) or equity (50%), while

Table 2.1 Descriptive statistics

Variable	Planning stage		Early start-up stage		
	Mean	Std. Dev.	Mean	Std. Dev.	Z-test
Debt	0.120	0.325	0.192	0.394	3.0***
Equity	0.061	0.240	0.204	0.404	6.3***
Patents	0.155	0.362	0.323	0.468	5.9***
Concept in development	0.296	0.457	N.A.	N.A.	N.A.
Concept developed	0.636	0.482	0.304	0.461	−10.0***
Prototype developed	0.068	0.252	0.260	0.439	7.7***
Start-up operation	N.A.	N.A.	0.390	0.488	N.A.
Product/service	N.A.	N.A.	0.046	0.209	N.A.
Business plan	0.601	0.490	0.835	0.371	7.9***
Serial entrepreneur	0.467	0.500	0.600	0.490	4.0***
International links	0.110	0.314	0.215	0.411	4.2***
Team	0.340	0.474	0.479	0.500	4.2***
House	0.587	0.493	0.625	0.485	1.2

Notes: All variables are dummy variables that take on the values one or zero. N.A. means not applicable. Z-test for the equality between two proportions
***Denotes significant at the 1% level

only one entrepreneur of this group relies on both, debt and equity. In the early start-up stage, 19% entrepreneurs rely on both sources of external finance while 73% choose only equity and 79% choose only debt.

The fraction of innovative nascent entrepreneurs, which includes those with a patent application or ownership of a business related patent, increases from 15.5% in the planning stage to more than 20% in the early start-up stage. An even stronger increase can be observed for the fraction of entrepreneurs who report to have developed prototypes. It is 6.1% in the planning stage and 25.2% in the early start-up stage. In the group of entrepreneurs in the planning stage, 66% applied for a patent or own one and 32% of these have also developed a prototype. In the early start-up stage, 155 new ventures have patents or have applied for patents, and 47% of these innovative start-ups have also developed a prototype. Although we do not know whether the patents are related to the prototype, it is likely that at least some of the nascent entrepreneurs try to protect their business relevant innovation (prototype) through patents.

As can be seen from the Table 2.1, 63% of the nascent entrepreneurs in the planning stage have developed a concept, while 30% of them are still in the process of developing a concept. As can be expected, the fraction of nascent entrepreneurs who have developed only a concept is significantly smaller for the group of nascent entrepreneurs in an early start-up stage. Most of them report "start-up operation" but only 4.6% have already launched a product or services. However, this is not surprising as these are start-ups that have not yet generated revenue.

There are also significant differences between both groups with respect to the fraction of those entrepreneurs who have written a business plan, who have established links with international partners, and who have previously started a business.

Table 2.2 Descriptive statistics: patents and sources of finance

	No external	Debt	Equity	Both	Total
	Planning stage				
No patents	299	40	20	1	360
	(85.4)	(80.0)	(80.0)	(100.0)	(84.5)
Patents	51	10	5	0	66
	(14.6)	(20.0)	(20.0)	(0.0)	(15.5)
	350	50	25	1	426
	(100)	(100)	(100)	(100)	(100)
	Early start-up stage				
No patents	229	49	34	13	325
	(74.1)	(67.1)	(43.0)	(68.4)	(67.7)
Patents	80	24	45	6	155
	(25.9)	(32.3)	(56.7)	(31.6)	(32.3)
	309	73	79	19	480
	(100)	(100)	(100)	(100)	(100)

Notes: Percentage in parentheses

In the group of incipient nascent entrepreneurs, these fractions are larger. Moreover, there are more serial entrepreneurs in this group and more team start-ups. The large fraction of teams (50%) is consistent with the prevalence of teams reported by the PSED.

Table 2.2 reports the number and share of nascent entrepreneurs who have chosen debt and/or equity finance for sub-samples of innovative (with a patent) and noninnovative (without a patent) nascent entrepreneurs. In the planning stage the fraction of innovative nascent entrepreneurs without external finance (14.6%) corresponds with their fraction in the total sample (15.5%). With respect to debt and equity they are slightly over-represented in this stage. In the incipient stage, however, they are under-represented in the category "no external finance" and they are over-represented with respect to equity finance. This points to a remarkable change in the capital structure between these early stages of the new venture.

One obvious explanation for the significant differences between nascent entrepreneurs in the planning stage and their counterparts in the incipient stage of launching a new venture is that at least some of the start-up characteristics may reflect the probability of making a transition a nascent entrepreneur in the planning stage to a nascent entrepreneur in the early start-up stage. Consequently, the fraction of start-ups with these characteristics would be higher in later stages of the start-up. Parker and Belghitar (2006) investigated the decision of nascent entrepreneurs to quit, to remain a nascent entrepreneur, or to start a new firm. They found, for instance, that preparing business plans and having experience in business ownership do not influence the decision by nascent entrepreneurs, while team ventures are less likely to make the transition from planning stage to launching the new venture. Another interpretation is that many nascent entrepreneurs may begin to write business plans, intensify their innovation efforts, or try to establish links to international partners once they have taken the decision to launch a new venture.

In summary, the descriptive statistics suggest that the decomposition of the sample into two groups is reasonable as both groups differ with respect to relevant business characteristics. In the econometric analysis, we will therefore investigate each group separately to test how innovative activity influences the capital structure of nascent entrepreneurs.

2.3 Empirical Results

2.3.1 Do Signals Affect External Financing?

In this section we will present estimates that are obtained from separate estimations of the MNL model for nascent entrepreneurs in the planning stage and nascent entrepreneurs in the early start-up stage. We did not differentiate between nascent entrepreneurs who rely only on equity finance and those who rely on both, equity and debt. Instead, we estimated the MNL model with the three categories "no external finance," "debt finance" and "both sources of external finance." For the group of entrepreneurs in the planning stage, this distinction would be unsuitable as only one entrepreneur has both debt and equity. For the other group, a Wald test of whether the two categories "only equity finance" and "both sources of finance" can be combined suggests that this is the case. Further, Wald tests reject the null hypothesis that these categories can be further collapsed, indicating that significant differences between the determinants of external sources of finance exist.[7]

A basic assumption of the MNL model is that irrelevant alternatives are stochastically independent from each other [Independence from Irrelevant Alternatives (IIA)-assumption], that is, the odds ratios in the MNL model are independent of the probabilities of other alternatives (Greene, 2003, p.724). Intuitively, the IIA assumption is not very plausible if nascent entrepreneurs view two alternatives as similar rather than independent. Therefore, we tested for the validity of this assumption. The results of a Hausman-test are reported in Table 2.3. The test results suggest that the null hypothesis of IIA cannot be rejected for both groups (planning stage, early start-up stage).[8]

The *marginal effects* of the explanatory variables on the probabilities of each category are reported for the group of nascent entrepreneurs in the planning stage and for the group of nascent entrepreneurs in an early start-up stage in Table 2.4. As can

Table 2.3 Hausman tests for the validity of the IIA assumption

Model	Omitted sources	$\chi^2(10)$	Evidence
Planning Stage	1	−5.409 (1.000)	For Ho
	2	0.071 (1.000)	For Ho
		$\chi^2(11)$	
Early start-up stage	1	−0.845 (1.000)	For Ho
	2	−5.401 (1.000)	For Ho

Table 2.4 Determinants of nascent entrepreneurs' external sources of finance

	Planning stage			Early start-up stage		
Variable	No	Debt	Both	No	Debt	Both
Patents	−0.019	0.028	−0.009	−0.105**	0.041	0.064
	(0.048)	(0.045)	(0.017)	(0.052)	(0.041)	(0.039)
Prototype devel.	−0.139	−0.021	0.160	−0.122*	−0.0335	0.155***
	(0.13)	(0.048)	(0.14)	(0.065)	(0.044)	(0.058)
Concept devel.	0.0192	−0.0547	0.036*	N.A.	N.A.	N.A.
	(0.039)	(0.034)	(0.020)			
Start-up oper.	N.A.	N.A.	N.A.	−0.037	0.036	0.001
				(0.055)	(0.042)	(0.043)
Product/service	N.A.	N.A.	N.A.	−0.211*	0.211*	−0.001
				(0.12)	(0.12)	(0.093)
Business plan	−0.095***	0.0558**	0.0394**	−0.0178	−0.056	0.074*
	(0.031)	(0.027)	(0.018)	(0.059)	(0.049)	(0.040)
Serial entrep.	−0.053*	0.0323	0.0202	−0.106**	0.060*	0.046
	(0.031)	(0.028)	(0.016)	(0.044)	(0.033)	(0.035)
Internat.links	−0.079	0.0346	0.0445	−0.116**	0.0094	0.107**
	(0.059)	(0.050)	(0.036)	(0.058)	(0.043)	(0.047)
Team	0.024	−0.0615**	0.0373*	−0.135***	−0.0616*	0.197***
	(0.033)	(0.026)	(0.021)	(0.046)	(0.034)	(0.037)
House	−0.094***	0.115***	−0.0215	−0.132***	0.114***	0.0178
	(0.032)	(0.028)	(0.016)	(0.043)	(0.032)	(0.035)
χ^2-statistic	60.48			109.9		
Pseudo R^2	0.122			0.128		
Actual Frequ.	350	50	26	309	73	98
Pred. Frequ.	373	39	14	334	71	75

This table shows the results of a multinomial logit estimations based on a sample of 426 nascent entrepreneurs in the planning stage and on a sample of 480 nascent entrepreneurs in the early startup stage
Notes: Multinomial Logit Estimation results. The standard errors are reported in parentheses. The asterisks *, ** and *** denote significant at the 10, 5 and 1% level respectively. The estimates reflect the marginal effects of a change of the respective dummy variables from 0 to 1

be seen from this table, having a patent or a prototype does not affect the probability of obtaining external finance if nascent entrepreneurs are in the planning stage. The estimated marginal effect of the dummy variable prototype on the probability of having no external finance is negative and the marginal effect of this variable on the probability of having both debt and equity finance is positive (0.16). However, the estimates of these marginal effects are statistically insignificant. The estimated marginal effects of the dummy variable patents are also statistically insignificant.

Other variables do influence the probability of being externally financed. Nascent entrepreneurs in the planning stage who have a business plan, who have started a business before, and who (or family members) own a house have a lower probability of having no external sources of finance. The probability of having debt finance is positively affected by the existence of a business plan and by house ownership. Obviously, the existence of collateral is very relevant for bank loans was as found by Ueda (2004). This can be seen as a timing problem that the entrepreneurs may first approach the bank and then if they fail, they prefer equity. In this case, it can be argued that banks do not recognize patents and prototypes as signals. But as Ueda (2004) shows, it is the entrepreneurs with low collateral who approach venture capitalists (VC). Therefore, it can be self-selection on the part of the entrepreneur that she/he chooses to approach the VC or business angel first. In this case we can expect that the entrepreneur directly approaches the VC/BA because she/he realizes that VC/BA might be the right signal receivers, and thus avoids banks altogether. Also, a business plan and a developed concept have a positive impact on obtaining equity. Moreover, being a team start-up reduces the probability of debt finance while it is positive for equity.

The results are strikingly different for the early start-up stage. Here, the probability of having no external sources of finance decreases if a start-up owns a patent or has applied for patent, has developed a prototype, has launched products/services, or has established international links. Again, serial entrepreneurs and team start-ups have a higher probability of choosing external finance. The probability of debt finance is higher if a start-up has launched product/services and as in the planning stage, team start-ups have a lower probability of debt finance and existence of collateral increases this probability. The probability of equity finance is higher for nascent entrepreneurs who have developed a prototype and who have contracted with companies or individuals outside the United States for goods or services. As in the planning stage, team start-ups and start-ups with a business plan are more likely to choose equity. The estimated marginal effect of the variable prototype is of the same order of magnitude as for entrepreneurs in the planning stage, but now this effect is statistically significant at the 1% level.

Note that estimated marginal effects imply that nascent entrepreneurs with prototypes have a remarkably higher probability of having equity finance. As the variable prototype is a dummy variable, the estimated marginal effect means that a nascent entrepreneur with a prototype has 16% higher probability of being financed by business angels or venture capitalists than other nascent entrepreneurs. In contrast, having a patent does not affect the probability of having equity finance.

The statistically insignificant effect of patents for equity finance might be explained by the fact that many start-ups with a prototype also report that they have applied for a patent or own a patent. Therefore, we performed additional estimations that take this into account by differentiating between start-ups that report only a patent, start-ups that have a prototype but no patent, and start-ups that have both.

The estimation results are reported in Table 2.5. For the group of entrepreneurs in the planning stage, the estimations results are hardly affected. For the group of entrepreneurs in an early start-up stage, however, the results now show that especially start-ups that report both, patents and prototypes, have a higher probability of being externally financed and in particular the probability of equity finance is positively affected. However, the results also show that start-ups with a prototype but no patent have a higher probability of equity finance, while this is not the case for start-ups with patents but no prototype. The magnitude of the estimated marginal effects is remarkable. It implies that a nascent entrepreneur who possesses a prototype

Table 2.5 Determinants of nascent entrepreneurs' external sources of finance

Variable	Planning stage			Early start-up stage		
	No	Debt	Both	No	Debt	Both
Patents/protot.	−0.140	−0.005	0.145	−0.272***	0.009	0.263***
	(0.13)	(0.057)	(0.13)	(0.080)	(0.057)	(0.081)
Only prototype	−0.121	0.0162	0.105	−0.0929	−0.067	0.160*
	(0.17)	(0.11)	(0.15)	(0.089)	(0.047)	(0.087)
Only patents	−0.020	0.035	−0.015	−0.077	0.016	0.061
	(0.052)	(0.050)	(0.017)	(0.065)	(0.048)	(0.054)
Concept devel.	0.019	−0.055	0.036*	N.A.	N.A.	N.A.
	(0.039)	(0.034)	(0.020)			
Start-up oper.	N.A.	N.A.	N.A.	−0.036	0.035	0.001
				(0.054)	(0.042)	(0.043)
Product/service	N.A.	N.A.	N.A.	−0.215*	0.216*	−0.001
				(0.12)	(0.12)	(0.094)
Business plan	−0.094***	0.055**	0.039**	−0.021	−0.053	0.074*
	(0.031)	(0.027)	(0.018)	(0.059)	(0.049)	(0.040)
Serial entrep.	−0.052*	0.032	0.020	−0.107**	0.061*	0.047
	(0.031)	(0.028)	(0.016)	(0.044)	(0.033)	(0.035)
Internat.links	−0.080	0.035	0.045	−0.116**	0.010	0.107**
	(0.059)	(0.050)	(0.036)	(0.058)	(0.043)	(0.047)
Team	0.025	−0.063**	0.038*	−0.137***	−0.060*	0.197***
	(0.033)	(0.026)	(0.021)	(0.046)	(0.034)	(0.038)
House	−0.094***	0.115***	−0.021	−0.135***	0.117***	0.019
	(0.032)	(0.028)	(0.016)	(0.044)	(0.032)	(0.035)
χ^2-statistic	60.58			111.1		
Pseudo R^2	0.122			0.129		
Actual Frequ.	350	50	26	309	73	98
Pred. Frequ.	373	39	14	334	71	75

Notes: Multinomial Logit Estimation results. The standard errors are reported in parentheses. The asterisks *, ** and *** denote significant at the 10, 5 and 1% level respectively. The estimates reflect the marginal effects of a change of the respective dummy variables from 0 to 1

and a patent has a 26.3% higher probability of being financed by business angels or venture capitalists than are nascent entrepreneurs without patents and prototypes. A nascent entrepreneur who has a prototype but no patent has a 16% higher probability while the estimated marginal effect of the dummy variable "only patents" is positive but much lower (6%) and statistically insignificant.

2.3.2 Robustness Checks

To check the robustness of our estimation results, we performed additional regressions using the subsample of nascent entrepreneurs in the early startup-up stage. Marginal effects based on the results of probit model estimations are reported in Table 2.6. Column (1) simply reproduces the results based on multinomial logit

Table 2.6 Probability of being financed by business angels and venture capitalists –
Results of Probit Estimation

Variable	(1) Equity	(2) Equity	(3) Venture Capital	(4) Business Angel
Patents/protot.	0.273***	0.271***	0.166**	0.228***
	(0.0764)	(0.0788)	(0.0662)	(0.0768)
Only prototype	0.174**	0.153*	0.126*	0.129
	(0.0831)	(0.0847)	(0.0713)	(0.0805)
Only patents	0.0717	0.0550	0.0135	0.0441
	(0.0563)	(0.0541)	(0.0198)	(0.0514)
Start-up operat.	0.00905	0.0186	0.0248	0.0357
	(0.0428)	(0.0426)	(0.0222)	(0.0409)
Product/service	0.00732	−0.0325	0.110	−0.0557
	(0.0976)	(0.0698)	(0.0913)	(0.0580)
Business plan	0.0783**	0.0774**	0.0145	0.0573
	(0.0397)	(0.0364)	(0.0150)	(0.0352)
International links	0.112**	0.111**	0.0123	0.101**
	(0.0497)	(0.0488)	(0.0171)	(0.0467)
Serial entrep.	0.0470	0.0277	0.00941	0.0455
	(0.0354)	(0.0356)	(0.0134)	(0.0329)
Team	0.201***	0.199***	0.0598***	0.154***
	(0.0368)	(0.0364)	(0.0196)	(0.0345)
House	0.0181	0.0145	0.0124	−0.00179
	(0.0358)	(0.0343)	(0.0131)	(0.0327)
Industry Effects	No	Yes	Yes	Yes
Wald test	$\chi^2(10)$	$\chi^2(20)$	$\chi^2(19)$	$\chi^2(20)$
	88.59	111.26	48.02	90.33
Pseudo R^2	0.1816	0.2335	0.2042	0.2070

Notes: Probit estimation results. Robust standard errors are reported in parentheses. The
asterisks *, ** and *** denote significant at the 10, 5 and 1% level, respectively

estimations reported in column ("Both") in Table 2.5. As can be expected, the results
are very similar. Column (2) contains the results of a probit estimation, including
controls (dummies) for industry-specific fixed effects.[9] The estimated marginal effects of the variables are hardly affected by the inclusion of industry effects. As
equity is used as a dependent variable, the previous results are based on the im-
plicit assumption that the probability of being financed by a venture capitalist is
affected by the same factors as the probability of being financed by a business angel.
However, there might be differences between venture capitalists and business angels. Column (3) reports estimation results, where the dependent variable takes the
value 1 if the nascent entrepreneur is financed by a venture capitalist, and Column
(4) reports on estimation results, where the dependent variable takes the value 1
if the nascent entrepreneur is financed by a business angel. Again, the results are
very similar. The estimated marginal effect of patents plus prototype is higher than
the marginal effect of patents alone. We tested for differences between the marginal
effects and the tests show that the differences are also statistically significant.

A problem of our approach might be the potentially endogenous dummy variables, prototype, and patents. One might consider the dependent binary variable "equity" as simultaneously determined with the dichotomous regressors "patents" and "prototype." If this were the case, our estimates would be biased because of endogenous dummy variables. Monfardini and Radice (2008) have proposed a test of exogeniety of a dichotomous regressor, which is based on the estimation of a recursive bivariate probit model. In our case, this model consists of a reduced form equation for the potentially endogenous dummy variable patents (prototype) and a structural form equation for equity. This enables a test whether the correlation between the residuals of these equations is zero, which is the null hypothesis (exogeniety).

To ensure that the other variables are exogenous, we included only the variable "team," which is very likely to be exogenous, and the sector dummies in our model. One might suspect that the variables "business plan" and "international links" which have a significant effect on the probability of having equity finance are also endogenous. A venture capitalist may force, for instance, nascent entrepreneurs to write a business plan or to have international links. Although we think that this is not very likely, we conservatively exclude these variables from the subsequent analysis. In principle, formal identification of the recursive bivariate model does not require additional exogenous regressors (instruments) if there is sufficient variation in the data (Wilde, 2000). However, Monfardini and Radice (2008) show that instruments are important because they preserve the validity of the LR testing approach in the presence of misspecification.

Therefore, we make use of two additional instrumental variables that do not have a direct influence on the probability of obtaining equity finance but do affect the probability of having patents and/or prototypes. In the survey, respondents were asked the following question: *"How important were these factors to you in the decision to start your business?"* Among others, two possible answers were *"Be innovative and in the forefront of technology"* and *"Develop an idea for a product."* Respondents were asked to assess the importance of the factors on a four point Likert scale. We used these scores to compute two dummy variables. The dummy variable "innovative" takes the value one if respondents assess being innovative as important or very important and zero otherwise. The dummy variable "idea" takes the value one if respondents assess development of product ideas as important or very important and zero otherwise. These two dummy variables are included as regressors in the reduced form equation for the dummy variable patents and prototype.

Estimation results are reported in Table 2.7. Columns (1), (2), and (3) report the results of three different estimations, where the potentially endogenous variable is patents, prototype or patents and prototype. As can be seen from the table, the estimated coefficients of these variables are positive and statistically significant. Moreover, the results of the corresponding LR-tests suggest that the null hypothesis of exogeniety of these dummy variables cannot be rejected at conventional significance levels. Hence, the results of the robustness checks confirm the previous estimation results.

Table 2.7 Results of Recursive Bivariate Probit

	(1a) Equity	(1b) Patents	(2a) Equity	(2b) Prototype	(3a) Equity	(3b) Prototype & Patents
Patents	1.167*** (0.42)					
Prototype			1.179** (0.52)			
Prototype & Patents					1.338** (0.58)	
Team	0.752*** (0.19)	0.452*** (0.13)	0.949*** (0.17)	0.0579 (0.14)	0.888*** (0.17)	0.269* (0.16)
Innovative		0.749*** (0.23)		0.707*** (0.26)		1.355*** (0.46)
Idea		0.839*** (0.24)		1.142*** (0.32)		1.072** (0.42)
Industry Effects	Yes	Yes	Yes	Yes	Yes	Yes
Likelihood-ratio test of $\rho = 0$	$\chi^2(1)$ 2.05697		$\chi^2(1)$ 0.779692		$\chi^2(1)$ 0.788504	

Notes: Bivariate probit model estimation results. Robust standard errors are reported in parentheses. The asterisks *, ** and *** denote significant at the 10, 5 and 1% level, respectively

2.4 Discussion and Conclusion

We developed two main arguments in this paper: First, *nascent entrepreneurs* who can signal appropriability and feasibility would be expected to have a higher probability of obtaining finance. Second, the stronger is the appropriability and feasibility mechanism, the higher is the probability of obtaining external finance.

Our empirical results suggest that innovative start-ups – with patents and prototype – are indeed more likely to be externally financed, especially by business angels and venture capitalists. It seems that technical knowledge per se does not have a positive influence on the mode of finance. A significant effect emerges only if patents are combined with the development of a prototype. One explanation for this result is that the development of a prototype reduces information asymmetries and resolves the problem of uncertainty associated with the *outcome* of innovation efforts. While prototypes may signal less risk, patents may signal that the nascent entrepreneur is well positioned to appropriate the returns from her investment in intangible assets. Hence, the expected value of an innovative new venture possessing patents and prototype may be more predictable than for innovative new ventures. However, we find this true mainly for individuals in the early start-up stage than those in the planning stage. This may suggest that investors react to signals from nascent entrepreneurs who have at least passed through the planning stage. This would also imply that the stress on prototyping/patenting begins right in the planning stage to obtain financing in the start-up stage.

The timing of patenting and involvement of investors is an issue. Are start-ups innovative before they are financed by external investors or do external investors make new ventures more innovative? The results of an empirical study by Hellman and Puri (2000), which is based on cross-section data on 149 Silicon Valley firms in the computer, telecommunication, medical, and semiconductor industries, suggest new ventures that follow an innovator strategy that have a higher probability of obtaining venture funding than firms following an imitator strategy. Hellman and Puri (2000) use ex-ante information to identify the different foundation strategies. Their results also suggest that innovators have a significantly higher number of patents than do imitators, which indicates that the "ex-ante intent is translated into a realized measure of innovation" (Hellman & Puri, 2000). Our results are consistent with this finding as nascent entrepreneurs who assess innovativeness and development of a product idea as important factors in the decision to start their business are more likely to apply for patents and develop a prototype. Using a sample of young German firms, Engel and Keilbach (2007) find that start-ups that possess patents before the foundation date are more likely to obtain venture finance. This indicates that many start-ups have patents before the involvement of the venture capitalist. We address the problem of endogeniety econometrically by estimating a recursive bivariate probit model, and the results of a test of exogeniety suggest that patents and prototypes are indeed exogenous with respect to external finance. It should be emphasized that the role of a prototype has not been investigated in the above-mentioned studies. Our results imply that the relevance of patents might be overstated by these studies because they do not control for the development of prototypes. Our study clearly indicates that a prototype itself is a strong signal and is especially strong when combined with a patent.

While a large literature has emerged analyzing the financial decisions of firms, virtually no study has yet been undertaken examining the financial decisions of innovative nascent entrepreneurs. Previous studies in the fields of economics and finance focused primarily on firm characteristics, industry characteristics, or macroeconomic effects. Few studies have considered the decision making by potential entrepreneurs that can ultimately lead to the start-up of a new venture and what the role of finance plays in shaping the process by which such new ventures are launched. Hence, this paper contributes to the existing literature.

The limitations as well as opportunities for future research can be observed in many aspects of this paper. We did not track individual nascent entrepreneurs over the start-up process, so that the empirical evidence is based on cross-sections of nascent entrepreneurs in the planning-stage vs. those in the early start-up stage. Availability of the data on timing of patenting/prototyping as well as obtaining finance remains a challenge. We tried to address this issue econometrically but it would be preferable to use a panel structure that exactly identifies the timing. Moreover our dataset needs more information on other innovation efforts of individuals, such as R&D activities, collaborations with other firms, or the role of public science institutions, as well as licensing activities. With respect to the financial sources, it would be ideal to have explicit elicitation of entrepreneurs' preferences, which may suggest a future research possibility.

2.A   Questions Used From the CIE Questionnaire

Defining and Identifying Nascent Entrepreneurs

- Which category best describes you? (Answer: Entrepreneur seeking capital to start a new business, Entrepreneur seeking capital for an operating business; Entrepreneur interested in business planning services or seminars; Visitor searching for general information about raising capital; Investor interested in investment opportunities; vFinance Investments Client; vFinance Employee or Associate)
- Are you actively involved in running this business? (Answer: YES/NO)
- What percent of this business do you own? (Answer: 0, 1–25, 26–50, 51–75, 76–99, 100)
- Did your business generate revenue in the first quarter of 2005 (January 2005 through March 2005)? (Answer:YES/NO)
- 2004 revenue. In US dollars? (Answer: Over 10 million, 5 million–10 million, 1 million–5 million, 500,000–999,999, 250,000–499,999, 150,000–249,999, 100,000–149,999, 75,000–99,999, 50,000–74,999, 25,000–49,999, 1–24,999, No revenue in 2004)

Distinguishing Between Planning Stage and Early Start-up Stage

- Which of these best describes you? (Answer: I currently own and operate a business; I am planning to start a new business; I am interested in private investments in businesses; None of the above)
- Where is your business in the start-up process? (Answer: concept in development, concept developed, prototype developed, start-up operation or product/service launched)

External Sources of Finance

- What sources of business financing have you already used to establish this business? (Answer: bank loans to the business, home equity loan in an owner's name, other bank loans in an owner's name, venture funds in exchange for stock/ownership in company, individual investors or companies in exchange for stock/ownership in company)

Business Characteristics

- Does your business own or have you applied for a patent that is essential to the business? (Answer: YES/NO)
- Has your business contracted with any companies or individuals outside the United States for goods or services? (Answer: YES/NO)

- Do you have a written business plan for your business? (Answer: YES/NO)
- Have you started another business before this business? (Answer: YES/NO)
- Do you or anyone in your household own your residence? (Answer: YES/NO)
- Which of the following best describes how your business was started? (Answer: A new business created by a single person; A new business created by a team of people; A business inherited from someone else; Purchase of an existing business; Purchase of a franchise)

Decision to Start the Business How important were these factors to you in the decisions to start your business? (Answer: very unimportant, unimportant, important and very important)

- Be innovative and in the forefront of technology
- Develop an idea for a product
- Fulfill a personal vision
- Lead and motivate others

Notes

[1] To the authors' best knowledge, there is no empirical study dealing with the role of prototypes for financial signaling.

[2] (*European Competitiveness Report*, 2006, p.91).

[3] Hall and Ziedonis (2001) find in their interviews with industry representatives that "stronger patent rights are especially critical to (the) firms in attracting venture capital funds and securing proprietary rights in niche product markets".

[4] If in case we think of secrecy as an alternative, the entrepreneur has to bear the cost of keeping the ideas secret.

[5] As with the usual signaling models, multiple equilibria are possible and generally several refinements exist to pin-point to one. For simplicity, we do not discuss the refinements and suggest that the intuitive criterion would suffice as it is possible that entrepreneur may still deviate from the pooling equilibrium, even if she is not sure of beliefs of other players. Intuitive criteria helps keep the most efficient outcome: low types are indifferent between acquiring appropriability/feasibility and acquiring nothing. See (Cho & Kreps, 1987) for intuitive criterion in signaling games.

[6] It is very intuitive to prove this as different appropriability mechanisms are possible, we consider these under a continuum with a ranking such that having a patent, and also a prototype is ranked highest against having only a prototype, only a patent or nothing, subsequently. The costs increase with the same order and therefore the value attached by the investor to the idea also increases, thus increasing the chances of obtaining finance.

[7] Test results are available from the authors upon request.

[8] This test compares the estimated coefficients of a model using all three categories and a subset where one of the categories is excluded. If the IIA assumption holds, then the estimation of the restricted and the unrestricted model should provide similar estimates.

[9] Dummies are 10 sectors.

Chapter 3
What Do Scientists Want: Money or Fame?

Scientists carry out the tasks of education, research, and commercial activities (*the so-called third task*) at universities. Despite their importance, the roles, motivations, and perceptions of university inventors have been relatively neglected topics of study. Most studies on university-industry relations have hitherto focused on a few selected elite universities, technology transfer offices (TTOs), patent legislations, or technology transfer activities in specific sectors from the United States. In these studies, the focus of interest is primarily the importance of institutions (patent legislation, policy mechanisms) and organizations (TTOs, university administration) in the patenting activities of scientists (see recent reviews by Siegel & Phan, 2005; Rothaermel et al., 2007; Göktepe, 2008). Some studies initiated the importance of individual oriented factors, but rather limited themselves only to entrepreneurial traits, experience, scientific background, and demographic factors such as age in order to analyze commercialization motives of scientists.

A number of studies (Gulbrandsen, 2004; Giuri et al., 2007; Meyer, 2005; Azoulay et al., 2007; Baldini et al., 2007; Bercovitz & Feldman, 2008) have recently paid attention to the roles of individual inventors in the university-industry technology transfer or academic entrepreneurship. In line with these recent developments, this research aims to focus on three factors of interest; namely, scientists' internal factors (e.g., human and scientific capital), external factors (directors – research group leader behavior, spin-offs at the institute), and psychological factors (perceptions, motivations). Within the scope of this paper we specifically focus on the relationship between the likelihood of scientists' patenting and inventing behaviors and their perception and presumptions on the benefits (measured in terms of financial benefits and/or scientific reputation) of commercial activities. We control for different socio-demographic as well as institutional factors and scientific fields in our analysis.

For this purpose, we use a unique database developed recently at the Max Planck Institute of Economics on the commercialization activities of over 2,500 scientists spanning over 60 different institutes constituting the Max Planck Society for Advancement of Sciences (hereafter referred to as MPG).

Using discrete choice models on patenting and invention disclosure to the MPG, we find that it is not money that influences these decisions, rather it is reputation/fame that drives scientists to both patent and disclose their inventions.

P. Mahagaonkar, *Money and Ideas: Four Studies on Finance, Innovation and the Business Life Cycle*, International Studies in Entrepreneurship 25,
DOI 10.1007/978-1-4419-1228-2_3, © Springer Science+Business Media, LLC 2010

Scientists' commercialization activities do not necessarily respond to monetary expectations. This confirms the assertions made by Long (2002) that patenting is basically an information transfer mechanism, and patentees use patents not always for the expected financial benefits by excluding others but for the nonmonetary benefits that accrue due to the information conveyed. Patenting activities could, to a certain extent, be independent from private economic incentives. This finding is important because it means that the academic capitalism is not essentially warranted. However, this does not mean that the design of intellectual property rights, other forms of incentives, in academic organizations would not have real effects on economic growth and productivity.

To observe the effects of motivation, our identification strategy also involved studying two different samples of noncooperating and cooperating scientists, respectively, in relation to industry collaboration. This identification strategy gives a straightforward test for assessing the effects of motivations by isolating the sample that entirely concentrates on laboratory activities for academic purpose, and hence how they drive patenting activities. Empirically, we show that noncooperating scientists who have more expectations to gain scientific reputation and visibility will more likely to patent. On the other hand, these scientists' commercialization activities do not necessarily respond to monetary expectations. The scientists involved in industry cooperations, however, seem to be not driven by reputational expectations and their patenting and disclosure activities might be more or less affected by the firm in context and its motives. The scientists may rather choose some other path of earning monetary gains than choose patenting because they expect patenting to benefit the firms.

The paper is organized as follows; the following section deals with the question of why scientists patent and disclose their inventions and takes the view of patents as signals that scientists use. In the third section, perceptions and motivations of scientists are shed light upon and propositions are put forward, after which in the fourth section the new dataset is introduced along with the variables of interest and methodology. The fifth section puts forward the estimation results and analysis, and sixth section concludes.

3.1   Why Do Scientists Make Invention Disclosures and Patent?

By the nature of their work, scientists constantly ask research questions and aim to show their research results in a timely fashion among their peers to achieve reputation and recognition (Merton, 1973). On the other hand, research results of scientists sometimes lead to invention disclosures and patents, which bring the economic incentives and pecuniary rewards into picture. The standard expectation is that patenting is an essentially economic phenomenon. It is almost generally believed that any invention would barely come out of a human's brain if that human did not have the possibility to earn all or part of the stream of economic rents that results from the industrial exploitation of his or her invention, a preliminary condition for that being that he or she ought to own a propriety right (usually a patent) over that invention (Schmookler, 1966). Inventive activity – along with technological change and the production of scientific and technical knowledge – was later on argued as something that was independent of economic needs and motivations (Rosenberg, 1974). More recent empirical findings also show that to some extent it is easier to accept that research and thus patenting is a matter of doing something professionally satisfying and rewarding (Gulbrandsen, 2004; Giuri et al., 2007; Baldini et al., 2007; Göktepe, 2008).

In line with these arguments, it is of particular interest to understand what matters for scientists to disclose their inventions to authorities and patent. Is it due to the perception of gaining reputation and free from pecuniary rewards? Yet, the question here becomes a little bit more complicated when we consider if the aim is to gain reputation and scientific visibility, why do scientists bother and patent instead of choosing the usual scientific publication route. We therefore alternatively argue that scientists' patenting activities might be different from their research activities and they are also motivated by pecuniary rewards in their patenting activities. The underlying model can be formulated as follows:

$$\text{Patenting/disclosure Activity} = f \text{ (motivations, age, gender, citizenship, career experience, research milieu).}$$

A further piece to this puzzle can be added by introducing if there is any significant difference regarding reputation and financial rewards between the scientists who patented and who had only disclosed their inventions to their employees. Inventing and patenting are two separable phenomena. It is accepted that not every invention can be patentable, even if scientists may have the expectations to patent. It is therefore accounting for the perceptions of scientists who actually applied for a patent with those who aimed but have not applied for a patent. Investigating and comparing what are the perceptions of scientists who patented and who invented would shed some light on the current debate on the role and ownership of intellectual property rights (IPR) at universities and public research organizations (PROs).

In what follows, we develop the principal arguments of this paper. We revisit some of the recent studies on the role of patents and why scientists patent. However, such findings merit further examination as they have been based on smaller samples or limited to a few selected universities or specific disciplines.

3.1.1 Patents as Signals

While many study why firms patent (e.g., Horstmann et al., 1985), very few studies concentrate on why do "individuals" patent. We tend to emphasize this due to the reason that benefits/costs that patents provide to firms might not be the same as for the individuals. Individual decision making is complex and one needs to first understand the specific functions that a patent provides to individuals. Common knowledge prevails that patenting is a mechanism to "privatize" information by excluding others to the intellectual property. At the same time, through the channel of patenting documentation, an individual may actually reveal the invention process. This, however, does not happen always.

Anton and Yao (2002) find that many of the patents do not actually reveal complete information on the invention process, therefore leading to "little patents–big secrets." So with this finding it seems plausible that monetary benefits to patents can be still assured, without a danger to the knowledge underlying the invention process. But do all individuals patent just because they want money by excluding others? Fame and money have always been the ultimate passions of humans mainly due to their effectiveness, their power to lure others, and their pervasive nature. The want for fame and money have always been omnipresent, in some cases omnipotent too. While we discussed about the monetary gains from patents, an equally intriguing gain is reputation. As we are interested in individuals, reputation seems to be another interest that would drive them to act on different things.

To be reputable, in the first place, information has to be conveyed about the person in context. In this view, a scientist can be thought of conveying "her type" (highly productive–low productive) to specifically two or more groups of people. One major group would be the compatriots in the research field concerned, while another can be the employer. To the first group, scientists have three ways to convey information about their type – either publish, or patent, or do both. To the second group one specific channel would be to report their findings, officially meaning, disclose their invention to the employer on an official basis.[1]

In this paper we focus on the channels of patenting and invention disclosure. Both of these can be viewed as information transfer mechanisms, not necessarily for monetary gains but for the nonmonetary benefits (Long, 2002) – in our case, reputation – that the individual foresees to be accrued. Individuals therefore would resort to actions that signal their type by conveying the right information to the concerned group. In a recent study, Jeon and Menicucci (2008) discussed the allocation of talent (brain drain) between the science and private sectors when agents value money and fame. They assumed that not only monetary rewards matter in agents decisions, but fame, which is defined as peer recognition, matters as well.

Although Long (2002) as well as the earlier studies by Schmookler (1966) and Rosenberg (1974) have long been debated in the academic literature, their logic applies primarily in the patenting context in general or in the context of industrial research and development (R&D) (e.g., Cohen & Levinthal, 1990; Eisenberg, 1987; Merges & Nelson, 1990; Merges & Nelson, 1994; J. Thursby & Thursby, forthcoming). We therefore investigated the role of financial rewards (by gaining monopoly powers/exclusivity) and/or the role of nonfinancial informational rewards (by reputation gain) as a driving force of inventing and patenting activities of scientists in public research organizations (similar to university context). By doing so, we move beyond the traditional argumentation of financial incentives are important for inventing activities for academic scientists. In the following section, we dig deep into what motivational factors (internal or external) are involved and how they get shaped and how they affect patenting/invention disclosure behavior.

3.2   Perceptions and Motivations of Scientists

In this section we mainly focus on the question, what are the perceptions and motivations of scientists, and their relation to commercial activities. To begin with we tip our hand with three basic assumptions that may motivate scientists to engage in research and commercial activities (Stephan & Levin, 2005): (i) An interest in solving the puzzle; (ii) an interests for recognition and prestige among peers; and (iii) an interest in achieving economic gains.

Solving the Research Puzzle: Puzzle-solving involves a fascination for the research process itself (Stephan and Levin 2005). Robert Hull (1988 in Stephan & Levin, 2005), a historian of science has described in detail the "puzzle-solving" aspect of research. In addition to Mertonian norms[2] (see Merton, 1973), there is considerable evidence that scientists have a desire for inventing (Stern, 2004). Scientists at universities are intrinsically motivated to do research. Much of the incentive to invent comes from the joy of solving research questions (S. G. Levin & Stephan, 1991; Stephan, 1996). Thus they are intrinsically motivated to conduct research, quite apart from the ability to earn financial rents from their effort (Stephan, 1996).

Recent empirical studies have also confirmed that the innate curiosity of scientists make them to do research that can be publishable. Gulbrandsen (2004), Giuri et al. (2007), Göktepe (2008) investigated the motives of inventors to patent. They asked whether monetary rewards or nonmonetary rewards were important motivations for patenting. Consistently, these studies although limited in scope found that personal satisfaction and doing something professionally enjoyable were important reasons for scientists to be involved in commercialization. They found that social and personal rewards (i.e., the fact that the innovation might increase the performance of the organization where the inventor works), personal satisfaction to show that something is technically possible, and prestige/reputation were considered by the inventors to be more important than other types of compensation like monetary rewards and career advancement.

Social and Personal Rewards: In addition to curiosity-driven research, scientists are motivated to achieve reputation and recognition among their peers in a timely fashion (Merton, 1973). Scientists are motivated by rewards of recognition and prestige among peers, and they have a strong interest in winning the game. Patenting can enhance the prestige and increase the scientific productivity of the scientists by reaffirming the novelty and usefulness of their research (Owen-Smith et al., 2002 and Owen-Smith & Powell, 2003). Although there is no explicit evidence that patents are used as a criterion to evaluate the academic merits of the scientists (e.g., in academic promotion), some scientists may consider patenting to increase their visibility and reputation. On the other hand, scientists who are concerned with more traditional academic values like open (public) nature of science might be less motivated to patent.

Source of Personal Income: Etzkowitz (1998) and Slaughter and Leslie (1997) underlined financial rewards, monetary compensation, and profit motive in their analysis of the new entrepreneurial scientist. Universities that provide greater rewards for scientists' involvement in patenting (e.g., in the forms of equity shares, royalty distribution) are found to motivate scientists to commercialize (patent) more. Greater rewards are measured by the amount of royalty income received by the inventor. Owen-Smith et al. (2002) argued that scientists' decisions to disclose are shaped by their perceptions of the benefits of patenting, licensing, and start-up company formation. The incentives to be involved in technology transfer are magnified or minimized by the perceived costs and gains of interacting with industry and TTOs. Siegel et al. (2003) concluded that organizational factors, in particular scientists' reward systems and technology transfer office compensation, influence the productivity of the technology transfer activities and thus the motivations of scientists to disclose their inventions.

Bercovitz and Feldman (2008) assumed that faculty members would be responsive to financial incentives and that there would be a direct relationship between licensing royalty distribution rates and the amount of technology transfer across universities. J. G. Thursby et al. (2001) and Lach and Schankerman (2008) provided empirical evidence that milestone payments and share of license revenues from their inventions are positively related to the motivations of inventors to patent. Markman et al. (2004) investigated the relationship between entrepreneurial activities and payments to scientists, departments, and TTO staff. They argued that scientists and their departments will be unlikely to disclose or participate in technology transfer activities unless they are given proper incentives to do so. They expect licensing revenues from technology transfer activities can motivate scientists and their departments towards entrepreneurial activities, given the scarcity of resources on research. Based on the arguments posed until now, we frame the following propositions for empirical testing. As we do not make a case only for reputation or only money drives patenting, we test several possibilities in terms of methodology. Apart from these following specific propositions, we also test several individual and external (institution specific) factors that affect patenting and invention disclosure decision.

- Scientists who expect high reputation are more likely to use both mechanisms (patenting and invention disclosure)
- Patenting and invention disclosure need not be necessarily driven by monetary interests

Individual and External Factors: The group of studies that focuses on individuals is inspired partly by psychology and behavioral sciences. These studies have focused on the socio-demographic characteristics of inventors. Macdonald (1984) and Macdonald (1986); Sirilli (1987); Amesse et al. (1991); Klofsten and Jones-Evans (2000); Giuri et al. (2007) investigated the characteristics, background, and socio-demographic features of inventors. The socio-demographic findings of these different studies are fairly consistent (see also Azoulay et al., 2007). Inventors were most often men; the average age being between 45 and 48. They were highly educated and had technical and commercial knowledge and had experience above the average.

Stephan and Levin (2005) investigated whether personal characteristics, age (life-cycle), citizenship status, gender, and receipt of federal funding were related to patenting behaviors. They found little evidence of age effects, yet they found that tenured scientists are more likely to patent than non-tenured ones (S. G. Levin & Stephan, 1991; Stephan, 1996). Women patent less than men, although the effect is smaller as the number of women employed in universities relative to men is low. In addition to the individual (socio-demographic) factors, one should also account for the perceptions of scientists on the use of knowledge (whether research should be open) and role of organizational factors, like the need for technology transfer office (TTO).

"A scientist, by choice of vocation, would heretofore have been assumed to have put aside all thoughts of business-like activity to live a monk-like existence as a searcher for truths about nature" (Etzkowitz, 1998). Etzkowitz continues – "attired in a white lab coat to protect their street clothing from chemical spills, the uniform of the scientist also signified a certain purity of motives, an abstraction from material concerns, and a bemused tendency toward absentmindedness in daily life." Further, "they were believed to find rewards for their discoveries not in pecuniary advantage but in recognition from their scientific peers through citation in the literature, election to a national academy, and the ultimate accolade of the Nobel Prize." J. G. Thursby et al. (2001) argued that scientists who specialize in basic research may not disclose because they are unwilling to spend time on the applied R&D required to interest business in licensing invention. They also stated scientists may not disclose because they believe that commercial activity is not appropriate for an academic scientists. Having this kind of perception or believing in the Mertonian norms of "disinterestedness," scientists would perceive that their research results should be freely accessible to any other scientists and businesses. Such scientists are also expected to be less interested in patenting or other commercial activities.

Scientists' incentives to be involved in technology transfer are magnified or minimized by the perceived costs of interacting with industry, TTOs, (Owen-Smith et al., 2002; Owen-Smith & Powell, 2003), or dealing with patenting, licensing, and company formation individually. Scientists who think the costs of commercialization, for example, patent applications, fees associated with starting a business, are very high will be less likely to get involved in entrepreneurial activities or patenting. Faculty decisions towards technology transfer are shaped by the institutional and organizational environments that are supportive or oppositional for university–industry technology transfer. It is therefore necessary to control for scientists' perception on the role of agents such as technology transfer offices.

3.3 Data Characteristics, Variables of Interest and Methodology

This paper is based on a large-scale survey of over 2,500 scientists in Germany aimed at obtaining information about the commercialization activities. The scientists pooled for this research are from the independent nonprofit research organization – the Max Planck Society for the Advancement of Science (MPG hereafter). MPG was founded in the late 1940s in Germany. The survey was conducted in the last part of 2007 at around 80 institutes specialized in different scientific disciplines and located at different cities in Germany. The MPG is funded to large extent by both the federal and state governments. Although the aim is to conduct basic research in the interest of general public in natural sciences, life sciences, social sciences and the humanities, the institutes takes up new and innovative ideas that the German universities are not in a position to conduct adequately. By providing equipments, and facilities, the research at the MPG complements the work done at the universities. Currently, the MPG has 4,300 scientists and substantial amount of graduate students, post-docs, research scholars, and guests scientists; 51% come from abroad. In 2006, the budget was around 1,379.1 million euros. 82% is from federal and state governments, while 13% is from projects supported by government, federal states, and the EU. Donations, evaluation royalties, etc. amount to 5%.

Different from the former university patent legislation (university teachers' privilege (section 42 ArbNErfG – Law on Employees' Inventions)), [organizational] ownership of intellectual property rights (IPR) regime has been valid since the 1970s. This regime has recently become a model of organizing property in university inventions as well (Buernstorf, 2006). The MPG has thus a well-established tradition of organized technology transfer, having established a dedicated technology transfer subsidiary in 1971 to promote technology transfer, and provide guidance, for example, patenting, licensing, and venture creation. Regarding technology transfer, MPG has a 100% subsidiary named "Max Planck Innovation," whose functions are mentioned as "within the Max Planck Society, the company provides the research institutes with advice regarding patent matters and organizes patent applications" and further "Its primary business is the transfer of patented and nonpatented technologies developed by Max Planck Institutes to industry and to negotiate and close license agreements."[3]

The survey was conducted by a professional consultancy company from October till December 2007. It was a telephone-based survey. Names of the participants were kept confidential and are not to be revealed. Previous studies on technology transfer, academic entrepreneurship, and available interview guides and questionnaires were consulted before constructing the survey. To check for possible interpretation errors and mistakes, pilot surveys were conducted with randomly contacted scientists from other public research organizations in Germany. In addition, the survey was proof-read. The survey has four parts. The first part is about invention, patenting, and research cooperation activities. Second part focuses on entreperneurial activities. The third part is about the perceptions of scientists on commercial activities in general. The final part deals with individual and professional demographic information (age, gender, academic title and education, citizenship).

Empirical Strategy: To construct the variables, we first concentrate on the variable of interest – patenting and invention disclosure. We use three groups of scientists to measure the relationship between likelihood of scientists' patenting activities and their perceptions and motivations to do so: scientists who have only applied for a patent, scientists who have only disclosed inventions to the MPG and not have a patent, and scientists who have both disclosed inventions to the MPG and also have applied for a patent. The set up for the econometric model therefore is of a multinomial discrete choice model; specifically, we use the multinomial logit estimation method. Measuring perceptions is a tricky issue. As our main propositions are on reputation and money, there are many ways that we could measure it. The questionnaire proved helpful at this stage as scientists were asked whether they expect commercialization (patenting results, research collaboration with private sector, consulting services, etc.) to increase their reputation based on a 5-point scale. In the same vein, the question on whether they expect commercialization to make money was asked. Using these two measures we constructed variables – "high money," "high reputation" if the respondents strongly agree with the prospects of getting money or getting reputation. As our interest was also to cover the demographic nature of the respondents, we have used age, gender (female or not), foreign-born scientist variables. These cover the aspects "internal" to the scientists. We further utilize data on their industry experience, MPG experience, the position (whether a director, a group leader, a post doctoral fellow), and which field of science do they belong. To clearly track the patenting and invention disclosure behavior one has to also account for the personal opinions of the scientists with respect to the nature and mode of commercialization. Scientists were therefore asked if they want their research to be open (free from exclusion) and if they think a technology transfer office (TTO) is indeed needed to take their research to industry or commercialize it in any other fashion. We utilize this information to account for the personal opinion of scientists about commercialization in general that may affect their actual commercialization behavior. The following section puts forward some statistics indicating on the nature of data, the variables considered, and the estimation results from the multinomial logit model.

3.4 Estimation Results and Analysis

After the necessary data adjustments, we had almost 1,100 usable responses. Out of this sample, 110 scientists reported only patenting, 99 reported only disclosure, and 187 reported both patenting and disclosure. Table 3.1 provides the descriptive statistics on the variables we consider. "P" denotes only patents; "ID" – only invention disclosures, and "PID" denotes patents and disclosures. The opinion based questions report numbers that respond to "highly agree and strongly agree" on a five-point scale. All others are particular numbers that pertain to the column category. It can be clearly seen that most of the scientists take both paths of patenting and invention disclosure, but only few of them do it for money. It is also interesting to see that scientists who consider their research to be freely available for everyone also patent and disclose inventions to MPG. The mean ages for every mechanism is around 40, while less than a quarter of scientists patenting, disclosing, or doing both is female. Almost half of the foreign-born scientists patent and the number is almost the same for disclosure, but lesser for both.

Table 3.1 Descriptive statistics on scientist patenting and invention disclosures

Variable	P(110) (Only patents)	ID (99) (Disclosures)	PID (187) (Both)
High financial benefits	28	24	37
High reputation	52	45	85
Open research	66	69	106
Commercialization costs are high	78	69	153
TTOs are needed	94	75	148
Age (mean)	41	40	44
Female	27	28	22
Foreign-born	42	40	49
Post-doc	38	22	32
Group leader	26	24	78
Director	5	8	26
MPG experience (mean years)	8.3	8.9	12.2
Industry experience (mean years)	1.1	1.2	0.7
Biology and medicine	50	46	105
Chemistry/Physics and other technical subjects	58	49	80

Source: Own compilation

P Only patents, *ID* Only invention disclosures, *PID* Patents and disclosures

Directors certainly seem to show a very high patenting and disclosing behavior, if not for each of them individually. There is almost an equal share of scientists patenting in the broad fields of biology and medicine compared to chemistry, physics, and other technical subjects. Post-docs and group leaders seems to show very high patenting and disclosure behavior. This may be due to their young age that they are needed to show performance mainly after PhD and therefore they might be more active in inventing and patenting.

Given this scenario, we estimated a multinomial logit model where all the three categories (only patent, only disclose, both patent and disclose) are considered. Table 3.2 provides the estimation results.[4] Based on our estimation results, we can observe that the scientists who expect high reputation from commercialization activities are more likely to perform both patenting as well as invention disclosure. This confirms our first hypothesis that scientists who expect high reputation are more likely to use both mechanisms. It can be interpreted as the scientists who would expect to have high reputation would signal it through patenting and disclosing their invention to reach the relevant audience who receive the signal. Second, we can see the effect is so strong that if scientists want reputation they do not necessarily take any one of the paths, but are very highly likely to take both.

Is money driving the patenting and invention disclosure behavior then? The answer seems to be no. As can be seen in Table 3.2, scientists in fact are less likely to take any of the three paths if their motivation is to gain money. The alternative path may be viewed as starting up for firms, consultancy, or just keeping it as secret for future monetary gains. This, however, we did not explicitly test, but we can confirm our second hypothesis that patenting and invention disclosure need not be necessarily driven by monetary interests. It is indeed reputation that drives these

Table 3.2 Multinominal logit estimates of reputation and financial benefits on inventing and patenting behavior of scientists

IND.VARS	P	ID	PID
High financial benefits	−0.790**	−0.559*	−0.796***
	(0.31)	(0.33)	(0.29)
High reputation	0.208	0.005	0.534*
	(0.33)	(0.32)	(0.28)
Open research results	−0.312**	−0.253*	−0.355***
	(0.13)	(0.13)	(0.12)
High cost of commercialization	−0.168	−0.328**	0.412*
	(0.17)	(0.16)	(0.23)
TTOs are needed	0.269	0.009	0.0106
	(0.19)	(0.16)	(0.16)
Post-doctoral fellow	0.558*	−0.0307	−0.501
	(0.34)	(0.39)	(0.4)
Group leader	0.479	1.159**	1.651***
	(0.49)	(0.49)	(0.39)
Director	0.685	1.117	2.115***
	(0.76)	(0.89)	(0.6)
Years MPG	−0.037	0.054*	0.037
	(0.03)	(0.031)	(0.024)
Foreign-born scientists	−0.145	0.155	0.620**
	(0.31)	(0.36)	(0.29)
Age	4.451***	−0.218	2.093**
	(0.97)	(1.23)	(0.92)
Female	0.141	0.16	−0.572
	(0.36)	(0.36)	(0.42)
Years work in industry	0.201	0.469**	0.125
	(0.2)	(0.2)	(0.19)
Biology and Medicine	1.69	0.441	2.230*
	(1.11)	(0.72)	(1.17)
Chemistry, Physics, and	1.565	0.412	1.784
Technical subjects	(1.1)	(0.71)	(1.17)
Constant	−19.46***	−1.043	−13.13***
	(3.58)	(4.48)	(3.57)
Observations	1074	1074	1074
R-squared	0.1892		
$P > chi^2$	0.00		

Robust standard errors in parentheses
The asterisks *, ** and *** denote significant at the 10, 5 and 1% level respectively
P Only patents, *ID* Only invention disclosures, *PID* Patents and disclosures

two, and scientists may view reputation as more important than money. Academic interests might be of more value to the scientists than monetary interests and this might be driven by the inner philosophy of science and want of basic research in order to solve the puzzle, answer the questions that are left unanswered, and other motivations.

This leads to the result on the opinion of scientists on research as being "open." Even though descriptive statistics show that there are a number of scientists who patent and disclose while having the view of open research, the estimation findings confirm their opinion. Scientists who consider research to be open are less likely to take any of the three paths to commercialization. Scientists who consider costs of commercialization to be high are less likely to disclose their inventions but are more likely to patent and disclose. If a scientist considers costs as high, she/he would not be willing to approach the MPG to disclose the invention in the first place, while if the research has high potential (may be through reputation), it might be possible that the scientist is willing to both patent and disclose.

Another interesting result is on the position variable. As a sequential process, the post-docs seem to be more likely to patent, the group leader is more likely to only disclose or take both paths, and the director would be more likely to only choose both paths. This might be possible due to the experience that each of these persons have by understanding the rules, regulations, and institutional culture of the MPG (i.e., existence of organizational ownership of patents and an active TTO since 1970s). It is as well as due to the fact that the personal responsibilities toward disclosing inventions may grow over time. This is confirmed by the MPG experience variable, that scientists having higher number of years with the MPG are more likely to disclose their inventions to the MPG.

On the demographics, it is interesting to notice that foreign-born scientists are more likely to choose both paths rather than only one of them, older scientists are more likely to patent and choose both paths rather than only disclose their inventions. Scientists with higher industry experience are more likely to disclose their inventions. Scientists in the field of biology and medicine, seemingly a very vibrant field with respect to inventions and patenting, are more likely to choose both patenting and invention disclosure. Being female is insignificant, which was expected as patenting and invention disclosure are indeed norms and practices of scientists in general and may not be particularly gender specific.

3.5 Collaborators Vs. Non-Collaborators

Is the negative sign an indicator that money does not matter or money is a disincentive? To further test if money indeed does not matter or is it a problem of interpretation on the negative sign of the coefficient, we run additional estimations where we divide the sample into collaborators and non-collaborators. There are strong reasons on why we do so and how will it matter to the analysis. we first concentrate on the motivations of scientists who already do not collaborate with industry in any form (joint projects, direct consultancy, etc). It is important to make this distinction due to many reasons. First, the choice to collaborate with academia may be an initiative driven by firm's objectives. Blind et al. (2006) show that German firms collaborate with academia for several strategic reasons. Mainly firms expect the patents generated from collaboration to leverage their own positions in negotiations with partners, suppliers, and the financial sector. Therefore, the scientific outcomes from a collaborative effort take shape of patents mainly because of the firm's interests, rather than of the scientists. Third, concentrating on noncollaborating scientists gives us a chance to isolate the sample to those who have never been involved actively in commercial activities and would be an ideal sample to test our hypotheses: what would drive those scientists to patent who were never before involved in commercialization activities? This identification strategy gives a straightforward test for assessing the effects of motivations by isolating the sample that entirely concentrates on laboratory activities for academic purpose, and hence how they drive patenting activities.

Another problem we address in these estimations is to avoid coding in terms of high-reputation and high-money, as that would give us access to also the opinions on the median and not just on the extreme. So we directly take the five-point opinion scale and include all the points from one to five rather than only opinions based on 4 and 5. Apart from sample size benefits, we would also benefit by the additional information and hence robust results.

We provide the estimation results for both cooperators and noncooperators sample. Table 3.3 provides the estimation results based on the noncooperators sample and Table 3.4 provides estimation results on the cooperators sample.

Non-cooperators Sample: Based on our estimation results in Table 3.3, we can observe that the scientists who expect high reputation from commercialization activities are more likely to perform both patenting as well as invention disclosure. This confirms our first hypothesis that scientists who expect high reputation are more likely to use both mechanisms. It can be interpreted as the scientists who would expect to have high reputation would signal it through patenting and disclosing their invention to reach the relevant audience who receive the signal. Second, we can see the effect is so strong that if scientists want reputation they do not necessarily take any one of the paths, but are very highly likely to take both.

Is money driving the patenting and invention disclosure behavior then? The answer seems to be no. As can be seen in Table 3.3, monetary expectations do not effect the patenting and invention disclosure activities of scientists. In the light of these results, our hypothesis that expectation of monetary gains affects patenting activity stands to be rejected. It is indeed reputation that drives these two and scientists may view reputation as more important than money. Academic interests might be of more value to the scientists than monetary interests and this might be driven by the inner philosophy of science and want of basic research in order to solve the puzzle, answer the questions that are left unanswered, and other motivations.

This leads to the result on the opinion of scientists on research as being "open." Even though descriptive statistics show that there are a number of scientists who patent and disclose while having the view of open research, the estimation findings confirm their opinion. Scientists who consider research to be open are less likely to take any of the three paths to commercialization. Scientists who consider costs of commercialization to be high are less likely to disclose their inventions but are more likely to patent and disclose. If a scientist considers costs as high, she would not

Table 3.3 Multinominal logit estimates of reputation and financial benefits on inventing and patenting behavior of scientists: Non-cooperators sample

IND.VARS	P	ID	PID
Reputation	0.0934	0.0254	0.499***
	−0.19	−0.18	−0.19
Monetary expectations	−0.214	−0.134	−0.161
	−0.18	−0.21	−0.21
Open research	−0.153	−0.177	−0.536***
	−0.18	−0.21	−0.18
High costs of commercialization	−0.108	−0.245	0.545
	−0.18	−0.22	−0.39
Need for TTOs	0.423*	0.0376	0.576**
	−0.23	−0.24	−0.29
Post doctoral fellow	0.446	0.296	0.277
	−0.35	−0.53	−0.53
Group leader	0.793	1.944***	2.232***
	−0.64	−0.65	−0.62
Director	1.402	3.104***	3.246***
	−0.85	−0.89	−1.11
Years in Max Planck	−0.0478	−0.0224	0.0503
	−0.04	−0.04	−0.035
Foreign-born scientists	0.516	0.502	0.312
	−0.37	−0.42	−0.37
Age (log)	2.428***	−0.129	−0.00615
	−0.9	−1.37	−1.63
Female	0.0461	0.0972	−0.940*
	−0.4	−0.43	−0.5
Years work in industry	0.102	0.365	0.183
	−0.25	−0.3	−0.32
Biology and Medicine	0.725	0.477	19.14***
	−0.82	−0.91	−5.77
Chemistry, Physics, and Technical subjects	0.558	0.653	18.19***
	−0.83	−0.86	−5.79
Constant	−13.70***	−3.135	−25.88
	−3.07	−4.89	0
Observations	1418	1418	1418
Pseudo R-square	0.17		

Robust standard errors in parentheses
The asterisks *, ** and *** denote significant at the 10, 5 and 1% level respectively
P Only patents, *ID* Only invention disclosures, *PID* patents and disclosures

be willing to approach the MPG to disclose the invention in the first place, whereas if the research has high potential (may be through reputation), it might be possible that the scientist is willing to both patent and disclose.

Another interesting result is on the position variable. As a sequential process, the group leaders and directors are more likely to only disclose or take both paths.

Table 3.4 Multinominal logit estimates of reputation and financial benefits on inventing and patenting behavior of scientists: Cooperators sample

IND.VARS	P	ID	PID
Reputation	0.0614	0.101	0.196
	−0.14	−0.15	−0.12
Monetary expectations	−0.244	−0.349**	−0.535***
	−0.16	−0.17	−0.12
Open research	−0.418***	−0.169	−0.333***
	−0.14	−0.14	−0.11
High costs of commercialization	−0.166	−0.26	0.178
	−0.18	−0.22	−0.19
Need for TTOs	0.316*	0.288	−0.0153
	−0.19	−0.18	−0.13
Post doctoral fellow	0.339	0.186	0.425
	−0.38	−0.4	−0.32
Group leader	0.188	0.207	1.440***
	−0.4	−0.41	−0.31
Director	0.361	1.224*	2.252***
	−0.82	−0.66	−0.56
Years in Max Planck	−0.00893	0.0470*	0.0531***
	−0.028	−0.026	−0.02
Foreign-born scientists	−0.123	−0.00732	0.0901
	−0.34	−0.34	−0.27
Age (log)	3.045***	1.044	0.413
	−0.96	−1.07	−0.74
Female	−0.0677	0.209	−0.761**
	−0.38	−0.36	−0.35
Years work in industry	0.235	0.594***	0.252
	−0.21	−0.19	−0.17
Biology and Medicine	18.35***	0.324	1.363*
	−3.35	−0.85	−0.75
Chemistry, Physics, and Technical subjects	18.62***	0.111	0.996
	−3.32	−0.85	−0.76
Constant	−30.88	−6.558	−4.615
	0	−4	−2.87
Observations	689	689	689
Pseudo R-square	0.15		

Robust standard errors in parentheses

The asterisks *, ** and *** denote significant at the 10, 5 and 1% level respectively

P Only patents, *ID* Only invention disclosures, *PID* Patents and disclosures

This might be possible due to the experience that each of these persons have by understanding the rules, regulations, and institutional culture of the MPG (i.e., existence of organizational ownership of patents and an active TTO since 1970s). If the scientists respond that TTOs are indeed needed for commercialization, then that positively affects the likelihood to only patent or take up both the paths. It is as well as due to the fact that the personal responsibilities towards disclosing inventions may grow over time. This is confirmed by the MPG experience variable that scientists having higher number of years with the MPG are more likely to disclose their inventions to the MPG.

On the demographic aspects it can observed that older scientists are more likely to patent and rather than only disclose their inventions or do both. Female scientists are less likely to choose both paths, and gender does not have an affect on any one of these paths exclusively. The subject-area effects of scientists are taken into account too.

Cooperators Sample: Table 3.4 presents the results on the noncooperators sample. As can be observed, the noncooperators are not affected by reputational expectations when patenting or disclosing their inventions. In fact, a striking result shows up on the monetary expectations variable. Scientists who expect monetary rewards to be high in commercialization are less likely to disclose or patent and disclose. A simple explanation can be found in the fact that they are cooperators with the firms. As mentioned before, first, the choice to collaborate with academia may be an initiative driven by firm's objectives. Blind et al. (2006) show that German firms collaborate with academia for several strategic reasons. Mainly firms expect the patents generated from collaboration to leverage their own positions in negotiations with partners, suppliers, and the financial sector. Therefore, the scientific outcomes from a collaborative effort take shape of patents mainly because of the firm's interests, rather than of the scientists. Scientists in cooperation agreements would very well know this fact and therefore, if they are driven by monetary interests, they might not choose the patenting path and look for other paths such as start-up activities or new product development that can be commercialized directly from the labs.

The results on open research seem to be also valid for cooperators, in that, the scientists who prefer their research to be openly available to others are less likely to patent or disclose. The need for TTOs affects the patenting activities positively. As with the cooperators, the group leaders are more likely to patent and disclose while the directors are more likely to only disclose and do both. Years of experience in Max Planck affects the likelihood of disclosures and choosing both paths positively. Age has a positive effect on patenting and female scientists are less likely to patent and disclose. Industry experience effects disclosure likelihood positively.

3.6 Discussion and Conclusion

In this paper, we are inspired by the tension whether the traditional assumption that financial rewards (gaining monopoly powers or exclusivity) are the main driving forces of inventing and patenting decisions of scientists. Or scientists' inventing and patenting activities are related to their traditional academic concerns, that is, gaining reputation and visibility. As we introduced earlier, this tension has been long debated in the literature especially in the context of industrial knowledge creation, protection, research and development (see Schmookler, 1966; Rosenberg, 1974;

Eisenberg, 1987; Merges & Nelson, 1990, 1994; Long, 2002; Cohen & Levinthal, 1990; J. Thursby & Thursby, forthcoming). We discussed this tension (money or fame) within the context of academic knowledge creation and research from the perceptions of scientists and their decisions to make inventions disclosures and patenting. Instead of making a case for or against one factor, we investigated both aspects. By doing so, we move beyond the traditional argumentation of financial incentives matter for inventing activities for academic scientists. This paper thus also contributed to the debate on the role of IPR and commercial activities at the universities and public research organizations.

Empirically, we show that scientists who have more expectations to gain scientific reputation and visibility are more likely to patent. On the other hand, scientists' commercialization activities do not necessarily respond to monetary expectations. By the same token, scientists' inventing activities are also related to their expectations of recognition and reputation while financial benefits are less important. Specifically, the scientists who expect high reputation from commercialization activities are more likely to perform both patenting as well as invention disclosure. This confirms our first hypothesis that scientists who expect high reputation are more likely to use both mechanisms. It can be interpreted as the scientists who would expect to have high reputation would signal it through patenting and disclosing their invention to reach the relevant audience who receive the signal.

On the other hand, scientists in fact are less likely to take any of the three paths if their motivation is to gain money. Invention disclosure and patenting activities could to a certain extent be independent from private economic incentives. It can be clearly seen that most of the scientists take both paths of patenting and invention disclosure, but only few of them do it for money. It is also interesting to see that scientists who consider their research to be freely available for everyone patent and disclose inventions to a lesser extent.

To observe the effects of motivation, our identification strategy involved studying two different samples of noncooperating and cooperating scientists, respectively, in relation to industry collaboration. This identification strategy gives a straightforward test for assessing the effects of motivations by isolating the sample that entirely concentrates on laboratory activities for academic purpose, and hence how they drive patenting activities.

Empirically, we show that noncooperating scientists who have more expectations to gain scientific reputation and visibility are more likely to patent. On the other hand, scientists' commercialization activities do not necessarily respond to monetary expectations. Scientists' inventing activities are rather related to their expectations of recognition and reputation while financial benefits are less important. Specifically, the scientists who expect high reputation from commercialization activities are more likely to perform both patenting as well as invention disclosure. This confirms our first hypothesis that scientists who expect high reputation are more likely to use both mechanisms. It can be interpreted as the scientists who would expect to have high reputation would signal it through patenting and disclosing their invention to reach the relevant audience who receive the signal.

The scientists involved in industry cooperations, however, seem to be not driven by reputational expectations, and their patenting and disclosure activities might be more or less affected by the firm in context and its motives. The scientists may rather choose some other path of earning monetary gains than choose patenting because they expect patenting to benefit the firms.

These findings are also important because it means that the academic capitalism is not warranted and traditional academic values seemed intact. However this does not mean that the design of intellectual property rights, other forms of incentives (e.g., accepting patenting activities as an academic merit, qualification for promotion or providing research funds to patenting scientists), in academic organizations would not have effects on economic growth and productivity. Controlling for a variety of other determinants, including age, gender, citizenship, scientific discipline, industrial and academic experience, scientists with high reputation perception from commercial activities are more likely to patent. We acknowledge that these factors (reputation and financial rewards) are not mutually exclusive, meaning that under certain conditions (in the long term) reputation and visibility of scientists may bring financial rewards maybe in the forms of research funds, if not personal gains.

Understanding of scientists' patenting decisions and behavior is still a recent phenomenon. Although only recently have some systematic studies started to appear, only few of them have examined the incentives and motivations of scientists' invention disclosure and patenting behaviors. This paper aims to open this discussion and interest further.

Notes

[1] Invention disclosure to the employer is a job requirement. Different from the former university patent legislation university teachers' privilege (section 42 ArbNErfG - Law on Employees' Inventions), [organizational] ownership of intellectual property rights (IPR) regime has been valid since the 1970s.

[2] Merton suggested four norms of science: universalism, communism (or communalism), disinterestedness, and organized skepticism.

[3] Source: Website of Max Planck Innovation; http://www.mpg.de/english/(accessed on 28/02/2008).

[4] A basic assumption of the Multinomial logit model is the Independence from Irrelevant alternatives (IIA)-assumption. Therefore, we tested for the validity of this assumption. We performed a Hausman-test and the test results suggest that the null hypothesis of IIA cannot be rejected.

Chapter 4
Regional Financial System and the Financial Structure of Small Firms

A large share of small business failures is attributed to financial structure misman-agement. Most of our knowledge on financial structure of small firms is from the streams of financial access and capital structure. The implications from capital struc-ture stream are threefold: (1) small firms are more debt based, (2) small firms tend to bootstrap their finances, and (3) small firms are more credit rationed. Beyond that it is well known in capital structure[1] research that owner, firm, and industry character-istics are important for these results. In the stream of financial access, research from the policy angle has been toward financial institution availability, rules and regu-lations, time for application, etc. The emphasis in this stream is mainly on banks and borrowers. The central message is that small borrowers have many problems in the access front mainly in developing economies. Until recently, these two re-search streams have been distinct from each other. Faulkender and Petersen (2006) unite these two in an effort to show that supply of capital is as important as demand for capital in determining capital structure choice of firms. It is still an open issue whether this result is applicable to small firms.

Geography of firm finance is mostly a black-box in economic geography as well as finance literature. This paper contributes by empirically testing for the effect of regional presence of lending institutions on different financing options utilized by SMEs. Not just utilization but how these are combined by SMEs is also analyzed. To do so, we introduce a modified measure of lending operational distance, which we call the "Commercial Operational Distance." This measure is calculated for both lo-cal as well as national lending institutions. Overall, we perform the analysis for two levels: rural and urban. The central question that we address is: how does regional commercial operational distance affect the usage and combination of finances.

Our results show that the presence of very local lending institutions affects the likelihood of urban small firms to combine retained earnings with either debt or debt and boot strap or debt, bootstrap, and equity. These combinations are not utilized by small firms that are in the regions where banks and semi-local lending institutions exist. They would rather depend on internal financing. For rural small firms, the presence of lending institutions does not matter. In fact, high presence of any lend-ing institution does not change the preference for internal finance. We also tested the effect of quantity channel that if all lending institutions are present in a region. High combined presence also does not deter small firms from using internal finance

P. Mahagaonkar, *Money and Ideas: Four Studies on Finance, Innovation and the*
Business Life Cycle, International Studies in Entrepreneurship 25,
DOI 10.1007/978-1-4419-1228-2_4, © Springer Science+Business Media, LLC 2010

both in rural and urban areas. The two reasons for these are that small firms may rely on internal finance as the quantity and price channels of lending institutions do not seem to work, and if they do work its only for very local lending institutions. The second reason might be that due to riskier firms approaching for debt, monitoring costs are pushed on to the borrower or credit rationing might trigger usage of internal finance only. In the case of small firms, Faulkender and Petersen (2006)'s proposition that usage of debt will increase with increase in suppliers of capital stands true only with respect to increase in very local suppliers of finance and not with all.

In the following section, we introduce the effect of source of capital on financial structure of small firms. In Sect. 3, we put forward the concept of regional financial system and provide our measure of commercial operational distance. Section 4 presents the data collection strategy and some initial observations. We then present the results of the estimated multinomial model for rural and urban firms in Sect. 5. We end this paper with discussion of results, conclusion, and directions for future research in Sect. 6.

4.1 Source of Capital and Financial Structure of Small Firms

Yet even 40 years after the Modigliani and Miller research, our understanding of these firms' financing choices is limited.
Stewart C. Myers[2]

While Stewart Myers makes a general remark on firm financing research, one can say that specifically in the case of small firm financing this remains true to date. In small firm financing research, progress has been made in terms of identifying the differences between small and large firm financing patterns (Bates & Hally, 1982), evidence of bootstrap financing (Auken & Neeley, 1996), and a lot of country studies have put further light into the subject. Two main aspects have been the focus of research on financing of small firms: (1) bank credit availability (as in Petersen & Rajan, 2002; Patti & Gobbi, 2001; Black & Strahan, 2002; Cowling & Mitchell, 2003, for example) and (2) capital structure and financing modes (as in Chaganti et al., 1995; Romano et al., 2001; Hutchinson, 1995, for example). These two aspects have been dealt on both start-ups and already existing small and medium enterprises.

The bank credit availability research has come up with many useful observations. Small firms are more reliant on relationship banking, but when there is lack of reliable information, lending terms become tighter (Baas & Schrooten, 2006). Black and Strahan (2002) find that deregulation of banking sector in the United States and wide-spread branch activities actually helped increase the number of incorporations. This also means that reduced monitoring costs due to diversification tend to play more roles to large banks than small banks, which rely on relationship lending. Does it mean that relationships do not matter? On the cost factor they certainly seem to. Berger and Udell (1995) find that banking relationships of small firms helped decrease interest rates on lines of credit. Petersen and Rajan (2002) observe that credit availability to small firms has increased as there has been a development in the financial sector.

While these results pin-point at the usage of mainly long-term sources of debt like bank loans, inherently they do not address the issue of other sources of financing. While failure of many small firms can be attributed to lack of credit availability, composition of firm's finances also plays a crucial role. The small firm capital structure research focuses on this point. Small firms need not respond to market assessments (Chaganti et al., 1995) and therefore could choose to finance themselves with the sources they deem to find useful or obtainable. In fact, as small firms are mainly owner-managed, the choice of financing is strongly influenced by preferences and goals of the owner-managers (Barton & Matthews, 1989, R. Levin & Travis, 1987 and Chaganti et al., 1995). Why is therefore an immense usage of debt finance? Hutchinson (1995) shows that equity aversion and the desire to retain control of the firm tends to restrain owner-managers from issuing equity. While the finance perspective of explaining capital structure decisions on firm's asset tangibility (as in the trade-off theories and Chung, 1993) and other firm characteristics, the corporate strategy perspective deals with goals, preferences, and motivations of entrepreneurs. Barton and Gordon (1988) suggest that the corporate strategy perspective is more efficient in explaining capital structure decisions of small firms. This might be true as the nature and operations of small firms are quite different from those of large firms.

Top management in order to retain their share of earnings would always prefer to finance the small firm using retained earnings rather than external credit or new stock holders (Chaganti et al., 1995). If the small firm has managers, then they tend to prefer debt and only external sources of financing. These results may seem important to existing SMEs. When one considers start-ups, the tendency towards financing is clearly equity mainly if the start-up is innovative (e.g., Audretsch & Weigand, 2005,Aghion et al., 2004), but at the same time younger firms perceive higher financial constraints (Binks & Ennew, 1996). As small and young firms perceive financing constraints and retain control, they have to limit themselves to using retained earnings. Bates and Hally (1982) finds that in the United Kingdom small firms tend to be more reliant on retained earnings and had lower liquidity and had rarely issued stock. If external financing was needed, they would prefer bank loans through the director.

Thinking in terms of strategic management perspective, financing choices relate to the owner's characteristics such as education, which are indicators of human capital which might be a substitute for financial capital but also helps in gaining financial capital mainly from sources of debt. In financial market literature, it is well known that younger people are more risk taking and hence might often get rejected for loans or directly approach equity providers. Such cases are quite too often in these times with examples from YouTube, Google, and ever increasing business plan competitions mainly targeting equity. Not just these characteristics, but also gender of the owner has also been found crucial in capital structure decisions.

While empirical evidence is disputed if women are more conservative and less-risk-taking in terms of financing, some studies throw a different light. Women tend to face unfavorable financing conditions more often than men (Riding & Swift, 1990), which makes them seek either equity or rely on internal financing. While Chaganti et al. (1995) finds this to be true, some contradictory evidence has shown up more recently. Orser et al. (2006) find that women business owners were as likely as men in seeking all types of financing, except for equity capital which women sought less than men. This evidence again is contradicted by Constantinidis et al. (2006) that gender effect is still present in financing options. These contradictions mainly seem to be due to country differences as these studies referred to women in different countries with different cultures. Yet another important focus of small firm finance research is that small family businesses are less likely to opt for equity and would rather run the businesses with retained earnings (for more recent research and a good review see Romano et al., 2001).

As can be observed, there are many factors that influence a small firms financing behavior and these factors are complex. As Romano et al. (2001) rightly note, the dynamic interplay between business characteristics and behavioral characteristics is important in financing decisions. These results also hold true for bootstrap financing literature, where small firms are found to bootstrap their financing needs with different types of financing like asset-based factoring, leasing and trade credit, or by using credit cards (Auken & Neeley, 1996). As Berger and Udell (2006) suggest, usage of these lending technologies by SMEs must be considered to avoid misleading conclusions that large lenders are disadvantaged in lending to SMEs and also this might help in understanding financial structure of more informationally opaque small firms. While there are other studies that concentrate on other topic such as the growth related features of small firm financing (Chittenden et al., 1996), the central message of all the findings are that small firms are more financially constrained, rely more on retained earnings, and combine bootstrap or short-term financing to their financial structure, which is more debt oriented. Evidence on women's preference is disputed while family firms are considered to be more reliant on retained earnings or debt. Given these findings, there is yet another important aspect that is to be analyzed for SME financial structure, which is the source of capital.

4.1.1 Source of Capital

Earlier work on capital structure concentrated mainly on owner, firm, and industry characteristics in the premise of information asymmetries, agency costs, and signaling. Only recently the concentration has shifted to the specific sources of capital. Faulkender and Petersen (2006, p.46) add that "The same type of market frictions that make capital structure relevant (information asymmetry and investment distortions) also imply that firms sometimes are rationed by their lenders." This indicates at the financial constraint the firms face and "thus, when estimating a firm's leverage it is important to include not only the determinants of its preferred leverage (the demand side) but also the variables that measure the constraints on a firm's ability to increase its leverage (the supply side)."

The supply of capital is as important as the demand factors on many fronts. Differentiated financial markets tend to originate when credit rationing is undertaken by banks. This also can be perceived as availability of bootstrap finance or financial innovation itself. The main competitive advantage of these new intermediaries is in collecting creditor information and decrease information asymmetry problems (Faulkender & Petersen, 2006). The one way that established intermediaries can decrease information asymmetry is by interaction with borrowers, relationship lending, etc. Small firms tend to rely mainly on short-term debt and therefore would ease their capital constraints if these new intermediaries are accessible. These firms also tend to be riskier ones. The use of debt capital, however, shall decrease as monitoring costs increase towards these riskier firms, and if monitoring does not help, then banks will resort to credit rationing. In both cases, firms tend to utilize lesser debt. Faulkender and Petersen (2006) shows that if debt levels are still found to be higher then it is due to the quantity channel where the number of lenders is higher or through the price channel where lenders compete on interest rates (mainly with local banks). Hence, every new source of debt capital will increase the usage of debt. Faulkender and Petersen (2006) operationalize this argument in the following manner, where Y_{ij} is the financing choice:

$$Y_{ij} = \alpha_1 \text{ demand factors}_{ij} + \alpha_2 \text{ supply factors}_{ij} + \epsilon_{ij}. \tag{4.1}$$

Faulkender and Petersen (2006)'s empirical strategy was to estimate leverage as a function of firm's capital market access (measured as having a debt rating). Given this measure is useful, it does not directly measure if the firm has direct access to capital markets. If financial markets are well integrated, that any firm could get money from any lender or any lender may provide credit to any firm in the economy, then this measure would suffice. In the following section we review the literature that this is not true and therefore we suggest using the source of capital as a regional measure. A small firm's capital structure composition may not just be a function of business and industry characteristics but also involves the supply of capital on the regional level. One must remember that small firms are not as mobile and do not establish their branches all over the country. They are very local and are crucial for the local economies. While the demand factors may say that small firms resist equity and use mainly internal finance or combine with other financing choices, the supply factors such as availability of financial institutions in the region may in the first place determine the composition of capital structure. If the quantity channel on the regional level is true, then firms will tend to combine more sources of finance that are debt-based or utilize the services of a lending institution, ceteris paribus. The same effect may be possible from the price channel. As we are talking of small firms, the financial structure takes a wider form including bootstrap financing (asset based lending, factoring, leasing). Most of these are lending technologies and need a presence of a lending institution. Hence firms may tend to combine these with internal finance if the quantity or price channels are not in operation. We therefore address the question of financial structure in terms of what other sources do small firms combine with internal finance.

Pollard (2003) puts forward an impressive review of literature to show that the field of firm-finance especially the small firm finance is something of a "black-box" in economic geography. Geography of finance, on the other hand, deals with the large international flows of finance and effects of monetary policies. Giving a geographical perspective to supply of capital would throw more light on capital structure decisions apart from only demand side determinants. In the next section, we review literature on geography of finance and how it matters to small firms. We then formulate measures of commercial operational distance of lending. While the empirical evidence mainly concentrates on the effect of operational distance on credit availability, innovation (Benfratello et al., 2006), lending growth, and household incomes (Shaffer, 1998), we focus the effect of operational distance on financial structure of small firms.

4.2 Geography of Firm Finance: Conceptualising Regional Financial System

The first question that appears in an economist's mind is that does geography really matter in financing firms? Klagge and Martin (2005) summarize the debate in this regard. The opposition to this notion is that good projects are always financed, no matter where they are, as long as risk-return profile is good. Also the problem is mainly considered as a demand but not supply based. Many banks were considered to view that regional demand is lacking. Finally, spillovers from other regions were considered to take care of the problem. Hence, money flows irrespective of geography. While these arguments seem to be convincing, some of the market-failure elements seem to be forgotten. As is well known, neoclassical finance theory assumes perfect capital markets, complete information and rational agents, while in reality they are'nt. Smaller regional financial centers tend to fulfill a complementary function on the client groups neglected by larger and international financial centers (Klagge & Martin, 2005). Also, financial capital usually gets attracted to an urban center rather than in the peripheries (Christensen, 2007).

Given that there are information problems between financiers and the financed, one might argue that financial intermediaries are necessary on the regional level for proper information flows, be it in the form of soft information or relationship based. This is certainly of importance to small firms as information costs and transaction costs are higher for small firms operating in regional level (Christensen, 2007). On the cost angle, monitoring and screening costs lower if banks are geographically closer to the borrowing firms (Petersen & Rajan, 1995). What about access to capital markets? While historically countries like Germany have tried establishing capital markets for small firms (Neuer Markt) it has generally been difficult for SMEs to access these. One main reason is that high listing costs make centralized capital markets inaccessible. These arguments might reinforce the point that at least for small firms, geography does matter in their financial access.

Small firms face high costs attributed to monitoring, screening, and information asymmetries from the lenders/investors. These costs increase with distance from the financial center (Pollard, 2003, Klagge & Martin, 2005, Chakravarty, 2006, (Christensen, 2007)). Therefore, to decrease these costs, regions have to be either closer to the center or make efforts to attract investors/lenders to their location. This situation gets even difficult in centralized financial systems (in this case, England) unlike in Germany where significant regional capital markets exist. Moreover it is a well-known fact that funding gaps are much more severe in economically lagging regions.

How does distance affect lending? First by reducing information asymmetries and second by banks resort to spatial price discrimination if they know the location of the borrower (Degryse & Ongena, 2005). Theoretically speaking, a monopolist firm charges higher interest rates to closer borrowers as they incur lower transportation costs in traveling to the bank branch. On the other hand, in order to address information asymmetry problems, lenders resort to costly verification through monitoring. Monitoring costs to the lender increase with the distance to the borrower. Hauswald and Marquez (2006) model that informed banks tend to charge higher interest rates to closer borrowers as the correctness of quality signals is lesser. Hence both positive and negative effects are possible due to distance. Empirically, (Degryse & Ongena, 2005) find that loan rates tend to decrease with the distance between the borrower and the lender, which confirms the information asymmetry. Small firms were found to be paying higher interest rates than large firms.

While these arguments are from the angle of information about the borrower, borrowers themselves tend to also have informational requirements. Convenience to reach the bank branch, reputation of the banks, quality preferences, and personal/long-term relationships tend to shape the borrower's preference for a particular bank (Elliehausen & Wolken, 1990). This might hint that borrowers might not have a regional preference for banks if their personal preferences are weighted higher. At the same time one might argue that the information about the above parameters actually increases when banks are located closer. Moreover, these preferences might be generalized to all kinds of banking relationships and may not apply for commercial lending. Lending systems tend to follow a cycle where each both lenders and borrowers gather information about each other, and transportation costs might actually limit the borrower's search space.

Given that a borrower's search space is geographically limited due to transportation costs, the only way to obtain a loan is by increasing a large number of banks in that limited space. Petersen and Rajan (2002) observe that credit availability to small firms has increased as there has been a development in the financial sector. Banks tend to reach to the clients through their branch networks and hence it is the reach and not monitoring ability that might increase credit availability. Following their logic, it would mean that more branch networks in a region would increase credit availability. If banks compete over interest rates, then more borrowers would compete for loans. The main problem with having many competitors is that lower-quality borrowers tend to obtain loans in a highly competitive market. Banks then resort to credit rationing (Petersen & Rajan, 1995) or charge high interest rates.

Financial constraints to small firms in the region would increase or decrease depending upon the number of sources of finance in the region and the type of competition between them. One way to understand the financial constraint situation is to concentrate on the financial structure of the small firms, which in a way, provides some inputs on how a region affects the combinations of different types of finance that are actually used.

4.2.1 Regional Financial System

Three arguments can be summarized for assessing a region's financial system (Klagge & Martin, 2005). First, Local critical mass of financial institutions and agents enables local institutions, SMEs, and investors to exploit the benefits of spatial proximity. Second, existence of regional capital markets may help to keep capital within the regions and hence into local economic development. Finally, in an integrated financial system, decentralized intermediaries increase the efficiency of allocation of investment (by fulfilling the information and networking function).

A Regional financial system can be conceptualized as a network of suppliers and buyers of finance for commercial purposes in a region of a country. To examine the role of a region's supply of financial capital, we first have to conceptualize it in terms of the actors involved. These actors are financial institutions/branches/agents active in the region, local/national Government financing initiatives, and initiatives from international bodies such as European commission, World bank focusing on flow of finance in the region. As buyers of finance in the present case are firms, we consider only seekers of finance for commercial purposes.

In this study, we focus on one element of the regional financial system, which is the lending institutions. In a centralized financial system, lending institutions (of intermediaries, to be specific) operate mainly through branch activity while being headquartered in a location, generally a financial center. We distinguish two types of lending institutions: local and national. In England, this trend can be clearly observed due to existence of building societies and credit unions on the local level and big banking groups on the national level. For matters of convenience, we shall call these local and national banks. Because of the increase in communication technologies, the geographical diffusion of banking technologies has increased, which decreases the operational distance between banks and borrowers. The current view of bankers is that as long as the local credit markets are competitive and integrated, operational proximities should guarantee flow of funds to local borrowers. However, is it really the case that utilization of financing sources is independent of locational characteristics of operational distance? Alessandrini, Presbitero, and Zazzaro (2008) summarize the importance of operational distance. First, closeness to borrowers enables banks to complement hard data with soft data collected on informal basis, which improves borrowers' screening. This leads to decrease in credit rationing (Williamson, 1984) and denial of credit (Zazzaro, 2002; Gehrig, 1998). Second, relationship-based banking increases the likelihood of loan approval due to competition amongst market entrants. Empirically some of these arguments are supported. Patti and Gobbi (2001) find that density of branches (relative to population) in a province increases the credit availability for small firms. Apart from benefits, the adverse effects that operational proximity poses is market power, leading to high interest rates and negative externalities. Because of multiple banking relationships, borrowers may reduce the hold-up problems but at the same time increases adverse selection problems. This is supported by empirical evidence by Degryse and Ongena (2005), who find in line with the results of Petersen and Rajan (2002) that, in Belgium, operational proximity led to higher interest rates. Increase in operational distance also gains importance as competition in local credit markets increases and as said before, transportation costs and information asymmetries explain why operational distance is important for financial constraints/credit availability in a region.

4.2.2 Measuring Operational Distance

One way of measuring operational proximity is in terms of operational distance. Though distance here does not mean kilometric distance, it means the distance of operations between banks and borrowers. Alessandrini et al. (2008) put forward the notion of operational distance as used in Patti and Gobbi (2001) by calculating the density of bank branches relative to the regional population. They use operational distance to show that share of smaller local banks in the region increases credit availability. Operational distance is measured by Patti and Gobbi (2001) as follows

$$\text{OPD} = \left(\frac{\text{Branches}_j}{\text{Population}_j} \right) \times 10,000,$$

where, OPD is operational distance that measures number of bank branches in region j per 10,000 population in that region. While this formulation measures the operational distance to general population, it is often used to measure financial constraints of firms as in Patti and Gobbi (2001). One problem with this is that banks' operations are aimed at providing services to all sections of the society and not exclusively for businesses. Population distribution might be not similar to the distribution of businesses in different regions. Therefore, as our motive is to consider the operational proximity to businesses in the region, we put forward our formulation based on number of businesses as the "Commercial Operational Distance COD)." Commercial operational distance calculates the branch density relative to 1,000 VAT businesses given by

$$\text{COD} = \left(\frac{\text{Branches}_j}{\text{Vat Businesses}_j} \right) \times 1000. \tag{4.2}$$

We calculate 4.2 for all the three types of lending institutions in the nine regions of England, namely East of England, East Midlands, West Midlands, North West,

North East, South West, South East, Yorkshire and Humber and London. Another issue is that, given that commercial operational distance is calculated separately for every type of lending institution, sometimes there might be competition between lending institutions, leading to similar behavior regarding branch location. Second, it is an interesting question to analyze what happens if a region exhibits high operational distance of all the lending institutions. While the COD formulation for each of the three presents commercial operational distance for each type of lending institution, we also inquire if COD of all the three together are required for improving credit availability and usage. Therefore, we calculate "combined commercial operational distance (CCOD)" as

$$\text{COD} = \left(\frac{\text{BS.Br}_j + \text{Bank.Br}_j + \text{CU.Br}_j}{\text{Vat Businesses}_j} \right) \times 1000, \qquad (4.3)$$

where Bs.Br_j, Bank.Br_j, and CU.Br_j represent branches of building societies, banks, and credit unions in the region j. In this manner, access to debt can be measured on a regional scale unlike in Faulkender and Petersen (2006). The next section puts forward the data and initial statistics.

4.3 Data and Initial Observations

The data requirements for such a study as ours are vast. At the outset, one needs firm-level data on financing, which is sampled on a regional level. For this purpose we use the United Kingdom Survey of Small and Medium-sized Enterprises' Finances (SMEF), 2004 sponsored by the Bank of England (Fraser, 2005). This survey provides us with a sample of about 2,000 small and medium enterprises in England. As Fraser (2005) notes, this was the first representative survey of SMEs to offer a close analysis of businesses with fewer than 250 employees, their main owners and their access to external finance. SMEs were defined as firms having less than or equal to 250 employees. The main topics that were covered in the survey included owner's personal characteristics, firm demographics, providers of external finance mainly commercial loans, assets and asset-based finance, credit cards, and equity finance. This survey allowed us to identify the specific combinations of finance that small firms used. This could be done by allowing the respondents to mark more than one option in the financing question. Hence specific combinations could be found as against having only internal finance. Firms had to answer if they had used internal finance (by using current/deposit accounts to run their business), equity finance (VC or friends, family, relatives), commercial loans, and bootstrap finance (which includes leasing, factoring, and asset-based finance, mainly short-term). Amongst 24 combinations that are possible, we concentrate on six specific cases. As our purpose is to identify the combinations of finance that are used as against having only internal finance, our natural choice was to consider the case of internal and all the

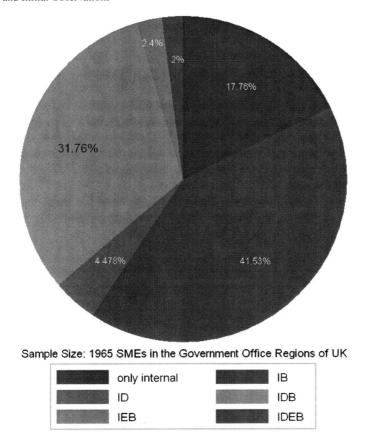

Sample Size: 1965 SMEs in the Government Office Regions of UK

	only internal		IB
	ID		IDB
	IEB		IDEB

Fig. 4.1 Combinations of Finance utilized by SMEs

mutually exclusive combinations that are used with internal finance. After removing the combinations that have less that 30 observations, we ended up with identifying firms that have only internal finance, internal and bootstrap, internal and debt, internal, debt and bootstrap, internal, equity and bootstrap, and all four kinds. Figure 4.1 shows the distribution of usage of these combinations in our sample.

As can be observed, almost 42% of SMEs combined both internal and bootstrap finance while 31% used internal, debt, and bootstrap. The next bigger share uses only internal (18%) followed by internal and debt (4.5%) and internal equity and debt (2.4%), and finally a very small share of firms combined all the four (2%). This hints that many firms have to limit themselves to using either internal and bootstrap finance. Also as observed in many countries, dependence on debt is higher. Only seven firms had VC-based equity and rest of the equity was from family or friends/relatives. As we are looking at combinations, every firm, theoretically speaking, can choose between combinations to be used. Inherently, each element of every combination has its costs and benefits, hence firms tend to make combinations of the financing sources in terms of the best cost/benefit choice possible. Recall the equation to be estimated:

$$Y_{ij} = \alpha_1 \text{ demand factors}_{ij} + \alpha_2 \text{ supply factors}_{ij} + \epsilon_{ij}. \tag{4.4}$$

Y_{ij} takes on values 0–6 depending on which of the seven mutually exclusive (see Fig. 4.2 for the exact categories).[3] alternative combinations of finance – only internal, internal and bootstrap (IB), internal and debt (ID), internal, debt and bootstrap (IDB), internal, equity and bootstrap (IEB), All the four (IEDB) – is chosen. This indicates at the usage of a multinomial logistic model with the base category as "only internal finance."

On the supply-side, our main focus is to calculate the operational distance of branches of lending institutions. As this is a regional measure, we consider

S12. And can I just check which of the following forms of finance you have used over the last 3 years for business purposes? **READ OUT – CODE ALL THAT APPLY**

		USER	NON-USER	DK
Internal	Current accounts (including personal accounts if used for business purposes)	1	2	3
	Overdraft (even if facility is there but has not been used)	1	2	3
	Deposit accounts (including personal accounts if used for business purposes)	1	2	3
Debt	Grants (A grant is a sum of money given to a business for a specific project or purpose. They are available from a variety of public and private sources including the government, the EU and some charitable organizations.)	1	2	3
	Commercial loans / mortgages from banks and other financial institutions (not including loans from friends, family or business owners)	1	2	3
	Leasing or hire purchase	1	2	3
	Asset based finance (including factoring, invoice discounting and stock finance. This is where a business sells its invoices and receives up to 90% of their value.)	1	2	3
	Credit cards (This includes personal or business credit cards used for business purposes. This means a card where you do NOT have to pay off the balance in full at the end of the month, not a store card. It also excludes debit cards)	1	2	3
Equity	Issuing shares (shares provide the investor with an ownership interest in the firm while providing the firm with cash or some other asset. It does NOT include any funds that the firm obtained from loans, or that must be repaid at some future date.)	1	2	3

(Bootstrap bracket spans: Grants, Leasing or hire purchase, Asset based finance, Credit cards)

Fig. 4.2 Categorization of financing options: original questionnaire format. Source: UK Survey of small business finances 2004

nine Government Office Regions (GOR) of England. GORs are standard statisti-
cal regions and administrative regions for policy purposes. Ideally we would have
preferred smaller regions but due to lack of data we limited ourselves to administrative regions. To measure the already existing financial environment, it will be
ideal to gather data of at least a year before than the data on finances. In our case
we therefore collected supply-side data for 2003 as the SMEF survey was conducted
in 2004. As discussed earlier, we use a modified version of operational distance (operational distance to businesses), which is based on the number of business rather
than population. Data about number of businesses is taken from the online statistics
section of the UK Statistics Authority.

There are three different type of lending institutions in England. First, the
national and widespread banking groups that operate all over England with more
than 6,000 branches all together. Second, the building societies that are semi-local
in nature but have long standing history of mortgage lending, dating back to mid
nineteenth century. Building societies operate through branches too but limit themselves to either the home-region (where the headquarters are located) or very nearby
regions. The third type of institution is the credit unions. Credit unions are very local. They are very specific to serving members, only in terms of loans and deposits.
Credit unions are very location-specific and rarely have any branches at all. Given
that the British banking system is very centralized, local lending institutions either
tend to play a complementary role in far off regions or have a long-standing history
and origins in the regions.

To calculate commercial operational distance, we needed to have region-wise
number of bank branches. It was difficult to obtain directly from each bank so we
obtained a list of banks operational in the year 2003 from the Financial Services
Authority.[4] We used this list, along with the post-code map of UK and traced the
number of bank branches for each post-code from internet navigation and mapping
sources such as www.upmystreet.com and www.locallife.co.uk. As the branch de-
tails referred to 2008, we then traced back bank branch closures and additions since
2003 using newspaper archives from internet and obtained the near-exact number of
bank branches in for government office regions of England as of 2003.

To obtain the building societies branch statistics, we compiled aggregate branch
statistics from the Annual reports of the British Building Societies Association[5] and
then visited each building society's website and categorized the branch addresses
into regions using the postcode map from the Royal Post. The Financial Services
Authority provided us with the aggregate annual reports of the credit unions in UK.[6]
Regional information on number of credit unions was readily available through
these reports. Figures 4.3 and 4.4 put forward maps of the composition of bank
branches, building society branches, and credit unions in nine Government Office Regions of England. As expected, London shares the highest number of bank
branches followed by the North West and South East. The North East and East
Midland regions are the ones having relatively low number of bank branches. East
Midlands fares the highest when it comes to Building societies bank branches
perhaps due to the long-standing history that building societies originated mainly
from this region. The North-West and South-East share similar patterns with East

Fig. 4.3 Composition of lending institutions' branches in government office regions of England

Midlands, while the North East has the least number of branches. The highest number of credit unions is found in North West followed by North East and the lowest number of credit unions are in the South East and East Midlands. Overall, marked differences can also be noted in terms of composition of different types of lending institutions in each region.

We calculated the commercial operational distance (COD) and combined commercial operational distance (CCOD) for each of the lending institutions for every

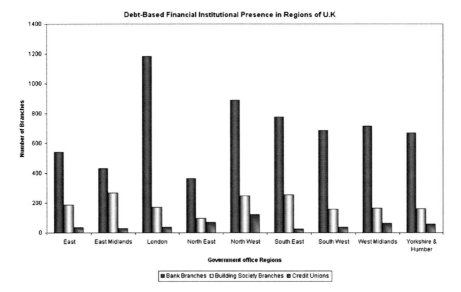

Fig. 4.4 Bar-graph showing composition of lending institutions' branches in government office regions of England

Table 4.1 Commercial and combined commercial operational distance variations in regions of England

Region	BS-vatbus	Bank-vatbus	CU-vatbus	CCOD
East	1.03	3.00	0.20	4.22
East Midlands	2.19	3.52	0.23	5.94
London	0.60	4.16	0.14	4.90
North East	2.15	8.15	1.60	11.88
North West	1.46	5.24	0.73	7.43
South East	0.90	2.75	0.09	3.74
South West	0.94	4.10	0.23	5.26
West Midlands	1.10	4.76	0.43	6.29
Yorkshire and Humber	1.25	5.30	0.46	6.97

region as in Eqns. (4.2) and (4.3), respectively. Table 4.1 shows that building societies are most proximate to businesses in East Midlands and the least proximate to businesses in London. Banks are most proximate to businesses in North-East and least proximate to South-East. Credit unions are most proximate in North-East and least in the South-East of England. When it comes to combined commercial operational distance, there are more lending institutions per 1,000 business in North East than any area while the least are in South East.

Bankers might argue that it is the demand problem and not supply that is responsible for financial constraints. To control for the demand problem, we use measures of financial literacy or capability. It might be possible that people in a particular region are more financially literate or attentive towards finance issues than other regions. This might be due to educational differences, significant economic events that happened in the region, motivations of people, or might just reflect cultural differences. One case is that if people live in a region like London where financial activity is all pervasive, they might follow the herd by being equally knowledgeable about finances or might rely on future availability of information and do not monitor financial markets frequently. People more distant to financial centers may monitor financial markets differently from the closer ones. As firms are owned and managed by such people, any analysis on their usage of finances needs to account for the amount of financial information they collect. To account for this information collection behavior, we utilize another random survey of almost 5,000 people in regions of UK. This survey is called the Financial Capabilities Survey conducted by the Financial Services Authority in the year 2004–2005. The survey aimed at knowledge of people in terms of financial matters and issues. We use a simple measure of information collection where the respondents are asked on number of financial areas they monitor, such as stock markets, inflation, interest rates, etc. By obtaining average number for each region, we get an approximate representative indicator of information gathering behavior of the people in each region. Figure 4.5 shows the degree of

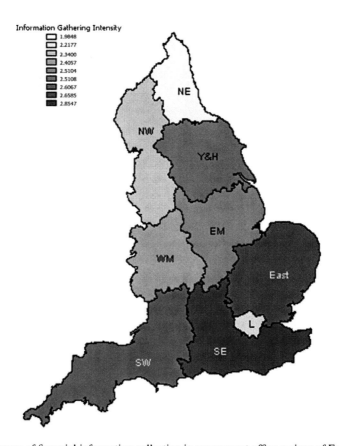

Fig. 4.5 Degree of financial information collection in government office regions of England

information collection in different regions. Out of 11 areas on which financial information could be monitored by people of nine regions, the highest average number of collection intensity was nearly three areas. While people in South-East, East, and South-West were amongst the highest monitoring, London and the North-East fared very low. This difference could affect the kind of financial combinations that firms could choose. This measure also accounts for the demand-side argument of bankers.

The demand side variables of capital structure that are considered in the Sect. 2 are firm age, asset-value, if the firm is family owned (>50% ownership), gender of the owner, owner's education, owner's experience and if owner participates in networking activities. As industries differ in capital structure composition, we also include industry dummies. In the banking and small firm literature, it is well known that rural firms are fundamentally different from urban firms and the level of financial constraints also differ. Equally, the operational distance might be very crucial for rural firms' financial planning. On the empirical side, this issue can be addressed by taking an urban/rural dummy, but in our dataset many of the variables like firm size, networking, assets were found to highly correlated to location. Hence, the better way to analyze this is to split the sample into urban and rural and then perform separate estimations for both. This has two advantages: (1) rural-urban difference can be better investigated and (2) special features affiliated to location come out very strongly without correlation problems. Hence we estimated eqn. 4.4 both on the rural and urban firms.

In Tables 4.2 and 4.3, we present descriptive statistics of both the demand and supply-based factors in the model for the sample of urban and rural small firms. While we discussed the supply side and information variables before, we shall now discuss the other demand side variables. The average value of assets of the SMEs in the urban sample is around two million pounds with a high variance amongst firms, while it is around 780,000 in rural firms. Both samples consists of youngest firms to very old firms,[7] which might indicate that the combinations of finance might show large differences between old and young firms.

Table 4.2 Descriptive statistics of demand and supply-side variables in equation in urban firms sample

Variable	Obs	Mean	Std. Dev.	Min	Max
Supply side					
BS-vatbus	1392	1.242472	0.51232	0.600348	2.190795
Bank-vatbus	1392	4.51337	1.432872	2.750609	8.151871
CU-vatbus	1392	0.433389	0.416871	0.091805	1.585706
CCOD	1392	6.18923	2.152599	3.739275	11.88163
Demand side					
Assets	1392	2327132	2.63E+07	0	7.96 (million £)
Firmage	1391	24.06614	32.89086	0	504
Owneredu	1392	4.471983	2.895609	1	9
Ownexp	1392	19.66056	11.15961	0	100
Info collection	1392	2.453266	0.224816	1.9846	2.8547

Table 4.3 Descriptive statistics of demand and supply-side variables in equation in rural firms sample

Variable	Obs	Mean	Std. Dev.	Min	Max
Supply side					
BS-vatbus	591	1.330701	0.493663	0.600348	2.190795
Bank-vatbus	591	4.263749	1.477431	2.750609	8.151871
CU-vatbus	591	0.40742	0.398676	0.091805	1.585706
CCOD	591	6.00187	2.141473	3.739275	11.88163
Demand side					
Assets	591	773928.3	2564375	0	3.40 (million £)
Firmage	588	26.2483	38.40965	0	504
Owneredu	591	4.038917	2.758071	1	9
Ownexp	591	22.1692	12.65039	0	58
Infor collection	591	2.532244	0.223957	1.9846	2.8547

Amongst urban firms the average education of the owners is Higher National Diploma/certificate level, which is equivalent to 2 years of university but less than bachelor's degree, which is similar in the case of rural firms. Owners in rural areas are on an average higher experienced than urban firms. Out of 587 rural firms, 22% were owned by female entrepreneurs, while amongst urban firms 16% were women-owned. In rural areas, almost 53% of entrepreneurs reported to be members of some networking organization while in urban areas it was 49%. Entrepreneurs in rural areas seem to be taking more part in networking activities, are majority owned by women, and are owned by much more experienced persons than in urban areas.

The demand-side variables reflect the vast differences between rural and urban firms, where urban firms fare well only in terms of asset-values but are equal or much inferior than rural firms when it comes to age of the firms, education, experience, gender distribution of ownership, and networking activities.

4.4 Empirical Results

We estimated (4.4) using multinomial logistic regression, where Y_{ij} takes on values 0–6 depending on which of the seven mutually exclusive alternative combinations of finance – only internal, internal and bootstrap (IB), internal and debt (ID), internal, debt and bootstrap (IDB), internal, equity and bootstrap (IEB), all the four (IEDB). The base category is "only internal finance." In this way we can compare the firms using other combinations than using only internal finance. The dependent variables of interest are our formulations of commercial operational distance as against the conventional measure used in Patti and Gobbi (2001). We performed the same regressions with the conventional measure of operational distance (with population as denominator) and find that it does not do as good a job as our measure in terms of explaining financial behavior of firms. Not only do the R^2 values increase, but also many variables achieve very high significance levels. Especially as our context is firms, one would realize that operational distance of lending institutions to firms is more crucial in financial situation of the firms than operational distance to entire population of the region. We then estimate equations based on our measure of combined commercial operational distance and put forward the results. We first discuss the results for urban firms and then for rural firms. All the estimated equations confirm to the independence of irrelevant alternatives (IIA) assumption that is required to be satisfied by multinomial logit. We used both Hausman and Small–Hsiao tests in order to test for IIA. All the combinations used have been found to be adhering to the IIA. This was expected as our coding of alternatives was mutually exclusive in nature.

Urban Small Firms: Tables 4.4 and 4.5 present the results of estimations on the urban sample. The variables related to commercial operational distance (COD) are COD of building societies ("BS-vatbus"), COD of banks ("Bank-vatbus") and COD of credit unions "CU-vatbus." The results show that urban firms in areas that have high building society COD are less likely to choose IB, ID, IDB, and IEDB combinations as against only internal finance. Similar results follow with banks in the case of ID, IDB, IDEB. The interesting component that actually increases the likelihood of choosing ID, IDB, IDEB is the credit union COD. This might imply that small firms in urban regions with high credit union operational distance tend to mainly rely on debt and combine the debt with either bootstrap or equity from family and friends. A main result is that it is the presence of very local lending institutions like the credit unions that actually increases the likelihood of obtaining finance other than depending on only internal finance. In the literature so far, this was theoretically predicted for rural firms, but our results show that it is also true for urban firms. While building societies tend to share a local history, firms may treat banks and building societies as the same as many of the building societies have often converted into banks due to similar functions.

Some more observations in Table 4.4 can be noted. As implied by the trade-off theories of capital structure, assets increase the likelihood of obtaining finance and firms tend to choose combinations of IB, IDB, and IEB. Older firms are less likely to choose IEB and IEDB. Family firms are less likely to choose IB, IEB, IDEB as against only internal financing, which is in line with the results of Romano et al. (2001). Female entrepreneurs are less likely to combine either internal with bootstrap or use all the four types as also found by Chaganti et al. (1995) and Riding and Swift (1990). Although statistically insignificant, female entrepreneurs are highly likely to combine internal and debt. Our analysis gives rise to some new and interesting results. Education level of the entrepreneur helps in choosing IDB and IEB as against only internal finance. Experience does not seem to help much in choosing other alternatives. In fact, highly experienced entrepreneurs tend to stick to internal finance rather than choosing ID, IDB, or IDEB. Networking efforts by the entrepreneur increase the likelihood of choosing IDB, IEB, or IDEB. Firms in urban regions that have people who collect high amount of information on financial sector tend to have a high likelihood to choose either IB or ID as against depending only on internal finance. There is significant difference in terms of industries, in that manufacturing, construction, and services are significantly different from agriculture.

Table 4.4 Effect of commercial operational distance on financial structure of small firms in urban areas (method: multinomial logit)

	IB	ID	IDB	IEB	IDEB
Assets (log)	0.122***	0.055	0.287***	0.347**	0.152
	(0.029)	(0.076)	(0.059)	(0.16)	(0.11)
Age of the firm	−0.0030	−0.001	−0.0057	−0.0410**	−0.0152*
	(0.0023)	(0.0040)	(0.0050)	(0.017)	(0.0087)
Family firm dummy	−0.461**	−0.146	−0.325	−1.458***	−1.419**
	(0.21)	(0.32)	(0.28)	(0.35)	(0.56)
Gender (female = 1)	−0.487*	0.231	−0.279	−0.763	−1.566*
	(0.26)	(0.72)	(0.26)	(0.64)	(0.93)
Owner's education	0.0680	−0.00142	0.0830***	0.165*	0.0515
	(0.044)	(0.052)	(0.019)	(0.088)	(0.099)
Owner's experience	−0.0208	−0.0583***	−0.0298**	−0.0379	−0.0655*
	(0.015)	(0.022)	(0.014)	(0.029)	(0.036)
Network-dummy	0.387	0.118	0.601**	0.876**	1.520***
	(0.26)	(0.43)	(0.25)	(0.36)	(0.25)
BS-vatbus	−0.369**	−1.386***	−0.294***	−1.537	−1.042***
	(0.14)	(0.21)	(0.11)	(1.08)	(0.25)
Bank-vatbus	−0.188	−0.531**	−0.492***	−0.126	−0.458**
	(0.23)	(0.23)	(0.18)	(0.61)	(0.20)
CU-vatbus	1.123	3.269***	1.966**	1.897	2.758***
	(0.95)	(1.00)	(0.83)	(2.73)	(0.74)
Info-collect	1.226***	1.544***	0.524	−0.325	0.622
	(0.33)	(0.23)	(0.42)	(0.81)	(0.50)
Services and trade	−1.853**	−1.153*	−1.399**	−2.377	−1.180
	(0.73)	(0.62)	(0.58)	(1.59)	(0.85)
Manufacturing	−2.025***	−2.105**	−1.546**	−2.226	0.110
	(0.70)	(1.00)	(0.67)	(1.87)	(1.07)
Construction	−1.553**	−1.325	−1.439***	−1.309	−0.562
	(0.74)	(0.83)	(0.55)	(1.72)	(0.66)
Observations	763	763	763	763	763
R-squared	0.31				

Base category: only internal finance
I Internal, *B* Bootstrap, *D* Debt, *E* Equity
Robust standard errors in parentheses
The asterisks *, ** and *** denote significant at the 10, 5 and 1% level respectively

The second estimation that was carried out was on the effect of the combined commercial operational distance (CCOD). Table 4.5 presents the results. While all other variables show the same signs as before, it is indeed interesting to find that the effect of CCOD is insignificant on choosing any type of combination. This makes our point stronger that presence of certain kind of lending institutions rather than all of them being present in a location. If we take results of Table 4.4, we can say that credit unions are very important in this regard. Herd behavior of banking presence therefore may not solve financial constraints. In a way, one can say that in urban areas no matter if all of the lending institutions are present, small firms still rely

Table 4.5 Effect of combined commercial operational distance on financial structure of small firms in urban areas (method: multinomial logit)

	IB	ID	IDB	IEB	IDEB
Assets (log)	0.119***	0.0500	0.276***	0.370**	0.149
	(0.029)	(0.075)	(0.058)	(0.16)	(0.11)
Age of the firm	−0.00309	−0.00144	−0.00540	−0.0436**	−0.0156*
	(0.0023)	(0.0042)	(0.0047)	(0.017)	(0.0092)
Family firm dummy	−0.471**	−0.170	−0.332	−1.480***	−1.434***
	(0.20)	(0.32)	(0.27)	(0.33)	(0.55)
Gender (female = 1)	−0.491*	0.227	−0.319	−0.746	−1.545*
	(0.26)	(0.73)	(0.27)	(0.62)	(0.92)
Owner's education	0.0660	−0.00765	0.0726***	0.176*	0.0460
	(0.047)	(0.049)	(0.019)	(0.091)	(0.094)
Owner's experience	−0.0205	−0.0559**	−0.0298**	−0.0345	−0.0641*
	(0.015)	(0.022)	(0.014)	(0.030)	(0.036)
Networking dummy	0.402	0.130	0.623**	0.846**	1.525***
	(0.25)	(0.42)	(0.25)	(0.36)	(0.25)
CCOD-VATBUS	0.0182	−0.0319	−0.0244	−0.0408	0.00536
	(0.064)	(0.088)	(0.070)	(0.15)	(0.080)
Information collection	1.013***	0.694***	0.174	−0.978	−0.0990
	(0.34)	(0.25)	(0.39)	(0.81)	(0.58)
Services and trade	−2.252**	−1.505*	−1.950**	−2.418	−1.571
	(1.01)	(0.90)	(0.86)	(2.26)	(0.99)
Manufacturing	−2.428**	−2.460*	−2.076**	−2.368	−0.265
	(1.01)	(1.27)	(1.04)	(2.56)	(1.37)
Construction	−1.943*	−1.643	−1.984**	−1.366	−0.949
	(1.05)	(1.04)	(0.87)	(2.49)	(0.85)
Observations	763	763	763	763	763
R-squared	0.30				

Base Category: Only Internal Finance
I Internal, *B* Bootstrap, *D* Debt, *E* Equity
Robust standard errors in parentheses
The asterisks *, ** and *** denote significant at the 10, 5 and 1% level respectively

on internal finance. It is less likely that they utilize other sources, if all of them are active in the region. This effect, however, might be due to many reasons specific to being an urban firm, which are yet to be investigated.

Rural Small Firms: Table 4.6 presents the estimation results on the rural sample. Unlike the urban firms, assets do not seem to significantly affect any choice. Older firms are less likely to combine all the four types of financing as against using only internal finance. Family firms too are less likely to combine all four types, internal and bootstrap and internal and debt as against using only internal finance. Female entrepreneurs are less likely to use IB, IDB, and IDEB as against only internal finance. Networking increases the likelihood to combine internal and bootstrap and these two with debt. The only operational distance measures that are significant are the building society and credit union COD. High presence of building societies

Table 4.6 Effect of commercial operational distance on financial structure of small firms in rural areas (method: multinomial logit)

	IB	ID	IDB	IEB	IDEB
Assets (log)	0.00725	0.125	0.167	−0.0178	0.368
	(0.090)	(0.17)	(0.11)	(0.14)	(0.28)
Age of the firm	−0.00478	−0.00102	−0.00133	−0.0390	−0.0436***
	(0.0031)	(0.0038)	(0.0025)	(0.026)	(0.015)
Family firm dummy	−0.875**	−2.182***	−0.610	−1.319	3.085***
	(0.36)	(0.74)	(0.75)	(0.88)	(0.85)
Gender (female = 1)	−1.088**	−0.259	−1.381***	−0.832	−42.48***
	(0.55)	(0.98)	(0.39)	(1.33)	(0.70)
Owner's education	0.0374	−0.105	−0.00990	−0.0720	0.000251
	(0.054)	(0.11)	(0.068)	(0.14)	(0.26)
Owner's experience	−0.00343	−0.0580	−0.0211	−0.0160	−0.0304
	(0.026)	(0.045)	(0.021)	(0.034)	(0.030)
Networking dummy	1.441***	0.400	1.287**	0.308	2.281
	(0.55)	(0.66)	(0.65)	(1.10)	(1.53)
BS-vatbus	−0.359	−3.038**	−0.0697	−0.259	0.340
	(0.31)	(1.25)	(0.18)	(0.39)	(0.38)
Bank-vatbus	−0.248	−0.620	−0.210	0.227	1.616
	(0.48)	(1.25)	(0.34)	(0.54)	(1.05)
CU-vatbus	1.575	1.899	0.515	0.170	−21.92**
	(1.73)	(3.58)	(1.41)	(2.13)	(9.04)
Information collection	0.944**	−5.165	0.154	0.598	−4.892***
	(0.41)	(4.18)	(0.63)	(0.77)	(1.59)
Services and trade	−0.377	19.89	0.392	−2.271**	2.866**
	(0.66)	(15.5)	(0.76)	(0.97)	(1.12)
Manufacturing	0.437	−22.20	−0.0647	0.608	3.839**
	(0.58)	(15.2)	(0.56)	(1.38)	(1.80)
Construction	0.129	20.12	0.231	−0.418	1.733
	(0.54)	(15.3)	(0.58)	(1.29)	(1.71)
Observations	261	261	261	261	261
R-squared	0.36				

Base Category: Only Internal Finance
I Internal, *B* Bootstrap, *D* Debt, *E* Equity
Robust standard errors in parentheses
The asterisks *, ** and *** denote significant at the 10, 5 and 1% level respectively

in rural areas relative to number of business makes it less likely that firms combine internal finance with debt. Similar is the result with credit union COD when it comes to choosing all the four types of finances. Information collection helps increase the likelihood of combining internal with bootstrap but decreases the likelihood of combining all four types. Table 4.7 presents the results based on combined commercial operation distance in rural areas. Unlike in the urban areas, CCOD seems to show a significant effect on usage of finance. Small firms in rural areas with high CCOD are less likely to use IDB and IDEB combinations.

Table 4.7 Effect of combined commercial operational distance on financial structure of small firms in rural areas (method: multinomial logit)

	IB	ID	IDB	IEB	IDEB
Assets (log)	0.00472	0.117	0.163	−0.0158	0.279
	(0.085)	(0.19)	(0.10)	(0.13)	(0.29)
Age of the firm	−0.00463	−0.000411	−0.00131	−0.0404	−0.0312***
	(0.0030)	(0.0037)	(0.0024)	(0.025)	(0.010)
Family firm dummy	−0.808**	−2.064***	−0.576	−1.280	3.872**
	(0.35)	(0.78)	(0.73)	(0.86)	(1.52)
Gender (female = 1)	−1.106**	−0.484	−1.402***	−0.873	−38.64***
	(0.55)	(0.88)	(0.41)	(1.30)	(0.68)
Owner's education	0.0399	−0.0762	−0.0103	−0.0723	−0.0151
	(0.056)	(0.12)	(0.068)	(0.14)	(0.26)
Owner's experience	−0.00388	−0.0566	−0.0209	−0.0151	−0.0200
	(0.026)	(0.041)	(0.021)	(0.034)	(0.023)
Networking dummy	1.439***	0.390	1.302**	0.346	2.310*
	(0.54)	(0.71)	(0.65)	(1.10)	(1.38)
CCOD-VATBUS	0.0155	−0.514	−0.0653**	0.132	−0.657***
	(0.047)	(0.43)	(0.030)	(0.088)	(0.21)
Information collection	0.539	−5.121	−0.00410	0.543	−3.569***
	(0.39)	(3.61)	(0.45)	(0.81)	(1.36)
Services and trade	−0.388	17.07	0.424	−2.305**	4.119
	(0.65)	(13.2)	(0.75)	(0.95)	(2.68)
Manufacturing	0.218	−21.87*	−0.0845	0.387	5.645***
	(0.51)	(13.0)	(0.58)	(1.35)	(1.78)
Construction	0.158	17.19	0.260	−0.471	3.384**
	(0.53)	(13.0)	(0.60)	(1.27)	(1.54)
Observations	261	261	261	261	261
R-squared	0.34				

Base Category: Only Internal Finance
I Internal, *B* Bootstrap, *D* Debt, *E* Equity
Robust standard errors in parentheses
The asterisks *, ** and *** denote significant at the 10, 5 and 1% level respectively

4.5 Discussion and Conclusion

The capital structure of firms is known to be different not only due to firm characteristics but also due to the sources of capital. Therefore, a need to understand the supply side effects on a firm's capital structure is warranted. A small firm's choice of financing sources may be limited by the supply-side financial endowment of the region. The main purpose of this study was to analyze the effect of source of capital on financial structure of small firms. Faulkender and Petersen (2006) puts forward the combination of both supply and demand sides of capital structure where the supply side is measured as access to debt via a rating. We put forward three reasons why this measure cannot be used for analyzing supply side and mainly for small firms. First, the supply of capital is spatial in nature. Second, small firms prefer proximate sources than distant ones. Finally, the quantity channels and price channels of lending might work more strongly in terms of space. We then put forward our concept of regional financial system, which is a way in which regions' financial endowments can be measured. As a beginning, we measure a component of the regional financial system, which is the lending institutions. Given that a rating might not be a right indicator for access to finance, we introduce the measure of operational distance and modify it as a commercial operational distance and find that it has higher explanatory power than the contemporary measures (Tables 4.8 and 4.9 provide the post estimation statistics of the regression using the COD measure).[8]

As a region's financial environment consists of very-local, semi-local, and national lending institutions, we calculated the commercial operational distance for each of these and find pronounced differences between the regions of England. These differences might indicate at the propensity of access to finance in each of the regions. Small firms are known to be heavily reliant on internal finance and the quantity and price channels are expected to drive usage of debt. We tested for the combinations of finance to the internal finance that small firms would utilize. Our findings on 2,000 small firms in England show that the quantity and price channels might work only for supply of very local capital. Firms tend to prefer internal finance when semi-local or national institutions are present. This result points out that semi-local and national institutions tend to drive away usage of debt due to monitoring costs or credit rationing, while very local institutions increase the usage of debt through quantity or price channels. Our results show that the presence of very local lending institutions affects the likelihood of urban small firms to combine retained earnings with either debt, or debt and boot strap, or debt, bootstrap, and

Table 4.8 Post-Estimation statistics for COD on urban sample

Log-Lik Intercept Only:	−1367.112	Log-Lik Full Model:		−949.286
D(693):	1898.571	LR(70):		835.654
		Prob > LR:		0
McFadden's R2:	0.306	McFadden's Adj R2:		0.254
ML (Cox-Snell) R2:	0.666	Cragg-Uhler(Nagelkerke)	R2:	0.685
Count R2:	0.474	Adj Count R2:		0.105
AIC:	2.672	AIC*n:		2038.571
BIC:	−2701.048	BIC':		−371.045
BIC used by Stata:	2363.179	AIC used by Stata:		2038.571

AIC Akaike Information Criterion, *BIC* Bayesian Information Criterion, *COD* Commercial Operational Distance

Table 4.9 Post-Estimation statistics for COD on rural sample

Log-Lik Intercept Only:	−467.649	Log-Lik Full Model:		−300.847
D(191):	601.693	LR(70):		333.605
		Prob > LR:		0
McFadden's R2:	0.357	McFadden's Adj R2:		0.207
ML (Cox-Snell) R2:	0.721	Cragg-Uhler(Nagelkerke)	R2:	0.742
Count R2:	0.521	Adj Count R2:		0.194
AIC:	2.842	AIC*n:		741.693
BIC:	−461.13	BIC':		55.911
BIC used by Stata:	991.21	AIC used by Stata:		741.693

AIC Akaike Information Criterion, *BIC* Bayesian Information Criterion, *COD* Commercial Operational Distance

equity. These combinations are not utilized by small firms, which are in the regions where banks and semi-local lending institutions exist. They would rather depend on internal financing. For rural small firms, the presence of lending institutions does not matter. In fact, high presence of any lending institution does not change the preference for internal finance.

One more question that we addressed is whether a combined presence of all the institutions increases the usage of debt through the quantity channel. We also tested the effect of quantity channel that if all lending institutions are present in a region. High combined presence also does not deter small firms from using internal finance both in rural and urban areas. The two reasons for these are that small firms may rely on internal finance as the quantity and price channels of lending institutions do not seem to work and if they do work its only for very local lending institutions. The second reason might be that due to riskier firms approaching for debt, monitoring costs pushed to the borrower or credit rationing might trigger usage of internal finance only. In the case of small firms, Faulkender and Petersen (2006)'s proposition that usage of debt will increase with increase in suppliers of capital stands true only with respect to increase in very local suppliers of capital and not with all.

This study was the first in a series of papers to include economic geography along with firm finances. The limitations of this paper lie in the choice of the size of regions, no direct elicitation of preferences of finance but rather usage. One of the main limitations is cross section nature of the data. We are trying to address this issue by collecting panel data on the key variables as part of a ongoing project. On the geographical angle we are going to obtain more detailed data where the zip code of the respondent could be identified and mapped to the branch zip code to obtain kilometric distances, which we were unable to do with this dataset.

The future possibilities are immense. The definition of regional financial system itself has components that have to be quantified and measured. Networks between financiers, borrower-financier networks, and the size of networks are crucial for measuring the total impact of a regional financial system. We are confronted with the global financial crisis, which will unquestionably result in the loss of jobs, real income, and an increase of financial constraints for small firms and individuals willing to start-up. In these kind of times, individuals tend to depend more on local resources and local communities. In this light, it is important to start introspecting on the strength of local financial systems.

Notes

[1] For small businesses we use the term financial structure since capital structure is essentially measured on a long-term basis while small businesses have often short-term financing agreements. Hence, by financial structure we mean long plus short-term financing.

[2] The Journal of Economic Perspectives 2001, vol. 15(2), p. 82.

[3] In terms of identification, once a respondent reports having internal and debt, that respondent is only counted for internal and debt and does not appear in other categories.

[4] http://www.fsa.gov.uk/

[5]htp://www.bsa.org.uk; We thank some of the building societies that have provided us data directly.

[6]http://www.fsa.gov.uk/pages/Doing/small_firms/unions/

[7]the oldest firms in both rural and urban sample were interestingly of equal age – 504 years, one in services while the other was in construction.

[8]Post-Estimation using comparative measures can be obtained from the author by request.

Chapter 5
Corruption and Innovation

While one strand of research views corruption as a boost to economic growth (e.g., Leff, 1964), the other views it as a hindrance (e.g., Mauro, 1995). Most of the "hindrance" literature relies on the linkage of corruption to growth through its affect on investment. Méon and Sekkat (2005) find that corruption affects growth independently from its impact on investment in economies where there are weak governance structures. There is a need therefore in this context to study channels of economic growth that are affected by corruption. This paper deals with one such channel, namely innovative activity. This paper is the first in a way that it tries to merge two distinct fields of economics of innovation and public choice.

Innovation is considered crucial for economic growth (mainly from the technology-gap approach, see Fagerberg, 1994). Innovative activities might get affected by corruption due to lack of resources or lack of trust in institutions. A related view is suggested by Shleifer and Vishny (1993) that corrupt firms would often report having advanced technologies, even though they are not needed necessarily. This would mean that the amount of innovative activity seems large only due to the presence of corruption. This issue is of utmost importance in the context of less developed countries (LDCs) that have to cope with socio-political-economic instabilities and bureaucratic pressures and yet at the same time have to keep up with economic growth.

The first contribution of this article is to provide analytical perspectives on the effect of corruption on innovative activities. There is meagre literature dealing with this directly. Veracierto (2008) puts forward a game theoretical model that shows the positive effect of penalties on corruption on product innovation but does not shed light on the exact channels or the direct effect of corruption. Therefore, for analytical purposes we try to use the "grease-sand" perspective of corruption and then apply it to innovative activities. The second contribution is to empirically investigate the assumption that corruption hinders innovation. We start with taking the approach of corruption as a barrier to innovation, but still maintain that not all kinds of innovative activities are affected negatively by corruption. Innovative activities that require exclusive use of public property (like permits, licenses) might get affected differently by corruption. This paper tries to contribute to the literature on innovation and public choice by exploring this issue by using a large-scale firm-level database, the World Bank Enterprise Survey conducted in 2004.[1] To test the grease/sand effect, we use the case of countries in the African continent where governance structures are often considered to be weak and therefore become a right set of countries to use. Using probit and instrumental variable probit models we find that corruption hinders product innovation and organizational innovation and has a positive effect on marketing innovation. Process innovation, however, does not get affected. The following section puts forward our analytical arguments for the grease and sand effect, Sect. 5.2 sheds light on corruption and innovation in Africa, Sect. 5.3 introduces the data and methodology. Section 5.4 provides the results and Sect. 5.5 concludes.

5.1 Corruption: Does It *Grease* or *Sand* the Wheels of Innovation?

Does bureaucratic corruption[2] greases or sands the wheels of innovation? Using the arguments generally applied to growth[3] leads us into two possibilities. One, that corruption is a barrier and two, that it is a boost to innovation. First we discuss the "grease the wheels" aspect where corruption is helpful for innovation. In order to do so, we build our arguments in terms of four dimensions.

First dimension: Innovative firms need faster approvals of permits, new licenses, and permissions to get new technology as fast as possible. If these have to come through a heavily bureaucratized structure, the time lag involved would ultimately cost the firms a market leading advantage. Such scenario can be viewed as a race between two symmetric firms needing permits for starting innovative activities or getting their innovative output in the market. The only difference we could assume is that of the ability to corrupt a government official handling the permit procedures. In this case, if the official allots permits to the firm that has a higher ability to corrupt, then it wins the innovation race and therefore a market lead. On the other hand, corruption could act as an incentive for bureaucrats to help fasten the process of getting the permits, etc. This argument follows closely in line with the formal model of Lui (1985). Mainly it can be seen as the need for government property on order to either launch innovative activities or to introduce finished innovative products into the market.

Second Dimension: When firms undertake or wish to invest in incremental innovation, corruption can act as a regular feature that a firm has to undertake to avoid any uncertainty. Corrupt firms can be certain that their requirements of permits, etc. will be granted as it can be seen that a long term relationship may exist between the corrupt firms and officials. Relationship corruption may therefore act as a facilitator for long-term planning and as an uncertainty reducing mechanism mainly in countries with sluggish administration and low monitoring levels.

Third Dimension: The third dimension is that of jumping the policy hurdle. Practice of the policy regulations by firms are limited to their discretion of whether it is perceived as harmful or beneficial. Policy makers need not always come up with the solutions that business owners think of best, rather there seems to be a gap between second best and best solutions that are undertaken. Bailey (1966) argues corruption allows private agents to adopt better solutions and override the ones provided by policy makers. On the other hand, in unfriendly governance systems, which do not allow much scope for innovation, corruption just might prove helpful for firms that would like to innovate and undertake entrepreneurial activities. Leff (1964) and Bailey (1966) view corruption therefore as a reaction to bad policies and hence jump the policy hurdle.

Fourth Dimension: The fourth dimension is that corruption as a facilitator to boost the scope and scale of investment as it acts as a hedge against political risks (Leff, 1964). Corruption may help avoid barriers to firms' planning of innovative activities by keeping away organized crime and vandalism.

These four dimensions lead to our running first hypothesis that Corruption affects innovative activity positively. Having discussed the four aspects relating to the grease the wheels of innovation argument, some problems can be associated with the above. First, are corrupt officials taking the right decisions? In lieu of corruption incentives, officials may resort to adverse selection where firms with good projects but having low bribing abilities may never get the needed permits. Second, in terms of relationship corruption, it is highly questionable that such long-lasting relations will keep away uncertainty as political stability and need for secrecy may only allow short-term dealings. So in this way a firm can never be assured of any future benefits from corruption from the same person. As these assumptions can be very well questioned, we turn to view arguments that put forward corruption as "sanding the wheels."

5.1.1 Corruption: "The Sand-the-Wheels of Innovation" Hypothesis

Apart from the usual suspects (Finance, networks, intellectual property framework, lack of skills, market-barriers) of barriers to innovation, the aspect of bureaucratic barriers cannot be ignored. Apart from long administrative procedures and restrictive laws and regulations (Acs & Audretsch, 1990), corruption may actually hinder innovative activities. Qian and Xu (1998) put forward a theoretical model to suggest that bureaucracy makes mistakes by rejecting promising projects and delays innovation. As discussed in the "grease the wheels" argument, if two firms are thought of in a race for permits, the loser cannot – as a result – initiate innovative activities. Second, if the financial markets were thought of as perfect, any loss to investment due to corruption costs could have been made up for. On the investment angle therefore, corruption can be seen as hindering R&D investment or early stage investments mainly in the presence of imperfect financial markets. Qian and Xu (1998) attribute to another aspect – namely the governance of the economy. In centralized economies, parallel projects involving high uncertainties are discouraged by bureaucracy. This is especially true if projects are government funded rather than private funded. A fourth aspect is that of deliberate delay. Government officials tend to delay granting permits, until they reach a threshold level of bribe that they can extract and/or wait until the maximum offer is made. This can act as a discouragement to firm, which would therefore prefer not undertaking any innovative activity. Hierarchical structure of bureaucratic decision making may also lead to delays (Myrdal & Fund, 1968) and subsequent increase in the total bribe payments. On the other hand, if many independent actors are involved, the cost of corruption gets higher (Shleifer & Vishny, 1993). In this case, the firm either chooses to undertake the cost or not take it at all. If it chooses to take the cost then the investment on innovative activities may get hit. In both the cases, the firm's optimal R&D is either not reached or never undertaken, making the firm stick to routinized activities in the industry it belongs to. Are corrupt firms innovative? not necessarily. Rose-Ackerman (1997) and Mankiw and Whinston (1986) put forward two ways in which low quality firms exist and enter the markets. First, the highest briber payer might just compromise on the quality of products, as the market existence is assured. Second, entry of a bribing firm might be detrimental to welfare. In these two cases, it can be argued that existence and persistence of corruption may very well hinder either innovative firms to continue innovation activities or firms to start innovative activities in general. All the above arguments also show that it is governance, institutions, and hierarchical structure of bureaucracy that hinders firms from either starting innovative activities or getting their innovative products to enter the markets. It can be quickly observed that activities that require public property explicitly are affected by innovation rather than the activities that do not, specifically activities within the firm. Thus the competing hypothesis would be that corruption affects innovative activity negatively. In the following section we put forward specific hypotheses related to the types of innovation.

5.1.2 Specific Hypotheses

Which kind of innovative activity does corruption affect in what way? A firm can be having more than one kind of innovative activity and not all of them might be affected by corruption at all! As we are interested in bureaucratic corruption, activities that require exclusive involvement of government (permissions, etc) might be affected and not necessarily the others. For streamlining our argument, we consider four distinct innovative activities undertaken by firms. We test the "grease the wheels" vs. "sand the wheels hypotheses" on the following four types of innovation (based on OECD classification; OECD, 2005).

Product Innovation: Product Innovation is defined as an introduction of a good or service that is new or significantly improved with respect to its characteristics and intended uses. To successfully enter the new products into markets, a firm has to undergo many stages of bureaucratic scrutiny. As the product is new, the government officials have to bear the cost of devising specific rules and regulations. They have to check if the firm complies with the present regulations. On the other hand, the firm has to therefore comply with all or many of the regulations, get necessary permits, etc., which increases its costs. A corrupt official may help speed up this process (the grease effect) or the firm may not be able to afford the regulatory costs and hence unwilling to invest in new products or introduce the new products to the market often (the sand effect). Hence the involvement of government officials/infrastructure leads us to the main hypothesis and its alternative.

- H1: Corruption affects product innovation negatively
- H1a: Corruption affects product innovation positively

Process Innovation: Process Innovations involve implementation of a new or significantly improved production or delivery method. This includes significant changes in techniques, equipment, and/or software. This is an internal aspect of a firm. Process innovations do not explicitly require government involvement. Therefore, one can expect that bureaucratic corruption may not affect firms' process innovation activity. Of course, the regulatory requirements may be concerned with how products are produced. An upgrade to present technology or introducing new technology which is already in the market cannot be affected by corruption as the value of the technology is well known (see Shleifer & Vishny, 1993 for an example). If the firm creates its own technologies for its own use, then it accounts for the present regulatory requirements in the process itself and therefore a corrupt official may find it difficult to find "loopholes" in order to seek bribes. On the other hand, some basic technologies have to be imported or require Government approvals to be used. In this case again, corruption might affect the pace of acquiring new technologies/equipment adversely. Hence we can hypothesize that

- H2: Corruption does not affect process innovations
- H2a: Corruption affects process innovations negatively

Marketing Innovations: Marketing innovations involve implementation of a new marketing method involving significant changes in product placement, promotion, etc. This involves getting new licenses. It is well known that corruption is mainly demanded from firms in this phase. Especially in countries with weak regulatory structures, getting a license becomes much difficult if bribes are not paid. Therefore, firms often tend to pay for bribes in order to get licenses. How far is getting a new license an innovation is a matter of debate, which is not much discussed in literature. For policy purposes, the OECD viewpoint is often taken. We modify it a little by considering if a firm is getting a license in order to enter a new market. To be consistent in our arguments and to account for major innovative activities, we keep the variable on marketing innovation.

- H3: Corruption negatively affects marketing innovation
- H3a: Corruption positively affects marketing innovation

Organizational Innovations: Implementation of new organizational method in firm's business practices; workplace organization and external relations come in the purview of organizational innovation. Getting a new external partner might not be easy especially in the context of semi-closed economies. Innumerable regulations, permissions, and large amounts of money involved make it a perfect avenue for bribing activities at every level. In the firms' point of view, corruption may help speed up the process, but if a firm cannot afford the cost (which is usually high in these cases), it might not undertake any such activity. Therefore, the effect of corruption on organizational innovation is quite confounding.

- H4: Corruption negatively affects organizational innovation
- H4a: Corruption positively affects organizational innovation

Inherently this can be seen as an empirical question in the context of relevant economy or a group of economies with similar socio-political and economic and cultural backgrounds. Empirically, the connection between corruption and innovation has not been undertaken yet. We contribute to the literature on public choice and innovation by suggesting that one of the channels that corruption uses to affect growth is through innovation. We initiate the process by looking into the ways in which corruption affects four types of innovation namely product innovation, process innovation, marketing innovation, and organizational innovation. We use the OECD definitions (OECD, 2005) for these concepts. The detailed definitions and measurement are provided in the data section.

In the following section, we shed some light on literature dealing with corruption and innovation in the African context. It is important to understand that in these days when Africa has been attracting a lot of external investment, one needs to consider the role of nonmarket elements like corruption and how they affect competitiveness of firms. Therefore, if any suggestion regarding competitiveness of firms in Africa has to be given, one has to account for the role of nonmarket elements.

5.2 Corruption and Innovation in Africa

African countries have been consistently identified as the most corrupt by the Transparency International[4] in terms of the corruption perception index. Shleifer and Vishny (1993) provide innumerable examples on how and in what forms corruption prevails in the continent. They put forward an interesting example that shows that in Mozambique, a bottle making factory had to resort to ordering a unique technology ten times the cost of the technology actually needed. This happened solely because secrecy can be easily imposed on transactions that are unique to the country while no alternate bids exist and therefore invoices can be inflated and everyone gets the share.

Mbaku (1997) puts forward an excellent historical perspective on reasons for high level corruption in Africa. The general view is that bureaucratic corruption in Africa is said to be a result of the weakness of the state. Incumbent regimes often shape their policies to cater the need of small business elite and thus may not be able to suit the common masses. It can be easily seen as to why entrepreneurship can face many hindrances in this case. Mbaku views that inefficiency and incompetence among civil servants as an important issue. "An important prerequisite for steady economic growth is an efficient civil service." Further, "the bureaucracy must be responsive to the needs of the entrepreneurial class in order to encourage and enhance innovation and productivity in the economy" (Mbaku, 1997, p.127). The most important fact is that African countries suffer with poor and ineffective enforcement of regulations, which encourages corruption. This corroborates with Shleifer and Vishny (1993), who view that this might pave way for distortionary effects. Apart from these reasons, chronic poverty, political instability, low literacy levels, and widespread income inequalities continue to be prominent reasons for corruption. Even though we can see that in the African context corruption may be a bad news for innovative activity, the arguments posed by Leff (1964) based on developing economies against this conclusion need to be verified too. Mainly studies in this line refer to benefits of corruption (see Mbaku, 1997 for a concise review in the African context). No evidence was found supporting the argument of formation of investible capital from corruption (Le Vine, 1975 for Ghana), as was the same with the argument of access to bureaucracy. The question whether corruption removes bottlenecks in the bureaucracy has not been tested specifically. Just as in other cases, in the African context too, a very few studies have been conducted to test the effect of corruption on economic growth and particularly with respect to innovation. The main obstruction has mainly been the lack of reliable data and usable measures of corruption for the continent.

5.3 Data and Methodology

Finding corruption data along with innovation is rare. The need to provide the interested parties in providing quality information on country investment climates led to the World Bank "Productivity and the Investment Climate Private Enterprise Survey." The data provides firm level information on investment climate depending on legal, financial, and social dimensions. Additionally, information on crime, corruption, and innovation is also provided. The data provide views of the respondents on these aspects and also information on the firm. This survey was conducted from 2002–2004 for different countries. The initial country sample consisted of Benin, Eritrea, Ethiopia, Kenya, Madagascar, Malawi, Mali, Mauritius Mozambique Nigeria, Senegal, South Africa, Tanzania, Uganda, and Zambia. Because of data completeness requirement, samples from Benin, Madagascar, Mali, Mauritius, Tanzania, Zambia, and South Africa were only considered. The sample size was 3,477 firms out of which 292 are from Madagascar, 84 from Mali, 157 from Malawi, 184 from Mauritius, 584 from South Africa, 184 from Tanzania, and 88 from Zambia. Because of the nature of the sample, all the firms were pooled and country effects were accounted for.

5.3.1   Variables and Empirical Strategy

As the main motive is to analyze the effect of corruption on four types of innovations, four different equations were estimated. The following is the description of the dependent variables and how they were measured. The dependent variable of interest is innovation. Innovation can be measured in different manners depending on what is being studied. In this paper, the focus is on the OECD manual on guidelines for collecting and interpreting innovation data that helps in measuring innovation (OECD, 2005). Broadly, innovations are classified into the previously mentioned four types based on the responses in the World Bank survey:

1. *Product Innovations*: Introduction of a good or service that is new or significantly improved with respect to its characteristics and intended uses. From the World Bank survey, this data is coded as binary from the questions on whether the firm has developed a new product line and/or upgraded an existing product line.
2. *Process Innovations*: Implementation of a new or significantly improved production or delivery method. This includes significant changes in techniques, equipment, and/or software. The process innovations can be intended to decrease unit costs of production or delivery. Process innovation was measured as a binary using response from the questions on whether the firm introduced new technology that has substantially changed the way the main product is produced and if a major production activity was outsourced that was previously conducted in-house.
3. *Marketing Innovations*: Implementation of a new marketing method involving significant changes in product placement, promotion, etc. Examples of marketing innovations include introduction or obtaining new product licensing. This was measured again as a binary from responses whether the firm obtained a new licensing agreement to operate in a new market.
4. *Organizational Innovations*: Implementation of new organizational method in firm's business practices, workplace organization, and external relations. This variable was measured also as a binary with response to the answer whether the firm agreed to a new joint venture with a foreign partner.

Although the OECD definitions have been widely debated upon, the Oslo manual has continuously adopted the critical changes that were suggested. For empirical purposes and suitability of data source, the OECD definitions have been used.

As this paper concentrates on bureaucratic corruption, corruption is measured as gifts or informal payments to public officials to "get things done" on an average as a percentage of sales. The variables regarding determinants and barriers of innovation were consolidated from different strands of literature. Even though the set of variables is very vast, only the stylized variables are taken into consideration here as the variable of interest is mainly corruption. Morck and Yeung (2001) provide a complete review of the economic determinants of innovation. The following are the stylized variables in the innovation literature – Firm size (e.g., Kamien & Schwartz, 1982; Acs & Audretsch, 1988; Scherer, 1992, Geroski, 1994), reinvested profits and problems with access to finance (Schumpeter, 1942; King & Levine, 1993;

Hall, 2002), technology transfer and networking effects (Love & Roper, 1999), human capital and skilled workforce, or technological change that is skill biased (Lawrence & Slaughter, 1993; Berman et al., 1994). The variables regarding technology transfer and networking effects were measured by questions on whether the firms use technology from clients or suppliers or develop in-house. Skill levels were measured by observing if the firm's manager is highly educated and if the firm has a highly educated workforce (in both measures high is measured as more than 12 years of education). Firm size is measured as three categories based on number of employees [small <20, medium (20–99), Large >10].

The following four relations are empirically tested:

- *Equation 1*: Product innovation as a function of corruption, reinvested profits, firm size, client technology, supplier technology, in-house technology, foreign ownership, financial access problem, and country effects were considered
- *Equation 2*: Process innovation as a function of corruption, reinvested profits, firm size, highly educated manager, highly educated workforce, financial access problem, foreign ownership, and country effects
- *Equation 3*: Marketing innovation as a function of corruption, reinvested profits, firm size, client technology, supplier technology, in-house technology, foreign ownership, financial access problem, highly educated manager, and highly educated workforce
- *Equation 4*: Organizational innovation as a function of corruption, reinvested profits, firm size, client technology, supplier technology, in-house technology, foreign ownership, financial access problem, highly educated manager, and highly educated workforce

As the dependent variables are binary in nature, discrete choice estimation methods were used. As there might exist an inherent endogeniety problem in the corruption variable that it might itself be a function of the success of the firm or any other corruption related behavior or the firm and its environment, first endogeniety was tested and then suitable instruments were used for each of the above estimations. The Wald test of exogeniety is then used to decide if the proposed model of endogeniety was the right decision to use. In the case of product, marketing, and organizational innovation, the null hypothesis of Wald test (that there is no endogeniety inherent) was rejected and that supports the use of instrumental variable model, while in case of process innovation and ordinary probit model was found to be sufficient. Instrumental variable probit (Newey, 1987) estimation was used for product, process, and marketing innovations, whereas probit estimation was used for process innovation. In the following section, some descriptive statistics and estimation results are presented. The instruments were chosen on three criteria:

1. That they are determinants of corruption.
2. That the instruments are not correlated to the dependent variables (innovation).
3. The model should be at least 80% specified after the instruments are introduced.

After these criteria were satisfied, the final instrument list includes sales to government, firm's perception of the efficiency of the government (Shleifer & Vishny, 1993), faith in judiciary, and taxes paid. Because of the rank and order condition requirement of instrumental variable estimation, the software STATA automatically uses all the other explanatory variables also as instruments for the instrumented variables. While using instrumental variables, a necessary condition is whether we have used the right instruments and if they are strong enough. There exist tests like Anderson–Rubin Wald test of weak instruments, Kleibergen–Paap test of under identification, Stock–Yogo weak ID test etc. We however could not use these tests as these are valid only for linear models and not for discrete choice instrumental variable models. Furthermore, there are no computably implementable tests for weakness of instruments in the context of models that use maximum likelihood method of estimation. Hence, we rely on the three criteria that we set. Our model leads to 85% specification strength and 76% sensitivity.

5.4 Results

Out of the sample of 3,477 firms, 1,289 firms report product innovations, 902 firms report process innovations, 93 report marketing innovations, and 81 report organizational innovations. Table 5.1 provides descriptive statistics of the variables of interest. As can be seen, there is much variation in the data. This might be due to country level differences. Table 5.2 provides some indicative country level statistics through which we can see that countries are different in many aspects. On an average almost 1.4% of sales is reported to have been given as bribes, the highest in Kenya and the lowest in South Africa. Government efficiency is relatively high in South Africa, followed by Mali and Senegal, the lowest being Zambia and Kenya. South Africa also leads in terms of faith in judiciary, least losses due to vandalism. Firms in Senegal, however, pay less in terms of taxes. Mali has the youngest firms while Senegal has many small firms. However, it has to be noted that in absolute terms all the countries except Kenya report similar views on judiciary, losses due to vandalism, and government efficiency.

Table 5.1 Descriptive statistics of variables in estimated equations

Variable	Mean	Standard Deviation
Corruption (percentage of sales)	1.38	5.5
Govt. Efficiency (low1-high 6)	3.08	1.27
Faith in judiciary (low1-high 6)	3.76	1.38
Losses due to vandalism (percentage of sales)	0.9	3.04
Firm size (number of workers)	140.1	404.8
Taxes (percentage of sales)	71.35	36.09
Firm age (survey year minus year of establishment)	20.97	19.6

Source: Own calculations

Table 5.2 Country-wise averages of variables in estimated equations

Variable	Kenya	Mali	Senegal	South Africa	Tanzania	Zambia
Corruption	4.41	3.16	0.44	0.12	0.63	1.42
Govt. Efficiency	1.89	3.43	3.22	3.56	3.17	2.11
Faith in judiciary	3.42	3.48	3.63	4.29	3.09	3.52
Losses due to vandalism	1.17	0.67	0.74	0.48	0.94	3.66
Firm size	146.5	41.35	56.28	237.29	99.88	145.15
Taxes	86.46	71.71	20.18	90.84	65.75	86.66
Firm age	27.26	12.6	16.01	24.63	18.2	23.55

Source: Own Calculations

Table 5.3 Country-wise maximum values of corruption as a percentage of sales

Country	Percentage of Sales
Benin	50
Madagascar	70
Malawi	30
Mali	15
Mauritius	66
South Africa	90
Tanzania	10
Uganda	29
Zambia	30

Source: Own calculations

Table 5.3 reports the maximum values reported as unofficial payments to government officials as a percentage of sales. The reported values vary a lot with the countries. The maximum reported values happen to be mostly in South Africa, while the least are in Tanzania. Overall, it can be seen that there is a high level of corruption amounts that reaches the government officials from firms. Especially in the countries where the frequency is high, the effect might be multifold. Table 5.4–5.7 report the four main estimations. The estimation strategy was to first estimate innovation dependent on the explanatory variables, controls, and country dummies, while instrumenting the corruption variable and then checking for the Wald test for exogeniety. Sales, asset size, industry common bribes, and sector dummies were considered as control variables in each estimation but none of these were found to be significant.

5.4.1 Estimation Results

Product Innovation: Table 5.4 presents the instrumental variable probit estimates of the effect of corruption on product innovation. An increase in corruption affects negatively on the likelihood for product innovation. Reinvested profits increase the likelihood of product innovation while problem with access to finance decreases the likelihood. Technology from suppliers and clients seems to increase the likelihood of product innovation. Coming to firm size, as is well known in other developing

Table 5.4 Effect of corruption on product innovation – iv probit estimates

| Explanatory Vars | Instrumented Var | | | |
	PRODINN	Corruption	athrho	Insigma
Corruption	−0.159***			
	−0.042			
Reinvested Profits	0.00222*	0.00943**		
	−0.0012	−0.0047		
Firm Size	0.319**	−0.176		
	−0.15	−0.25		
Ownership	−0.164	−0.345		
	−0.12	−0.42		
Client_tech	0.242	−0.819*		
	−0.2	−0.43		
Supp_tech	0.238*	−0.118		
	−0.14	−0.39		
Inhousetech	0.312*	−0.291		
	−0.18	−0.38		
Financial Access Problem	−0.524***	−2.433***		
	−0.11	−0.32		
Multiple Businesses		3.738		
		−4.44		
Sales to Govt.		−0.0104		
		−0.0091		
Efficiency of Govt. (low-high)		0.0856		
		−0.13		
Faith in Judiciary		−0.252**		
		−0.13		
Quality Certification		−0.652*		
		−0.35		
Taxes Paid		−0.0119**		
		−0.0055		
Benin	0.838***	4.480***		
	−0.27	−0.74		
Madagascar	0.102	0.927*		
	−0.17	−0.56		
Mali	−0.0887	1.082		
	−0.26	−0.8		
Mauritius	0.0349	0.54		
	−0.17	−0.63		
Tanzania	−0.0224	−0.465		
	−0.19	−0.74		
Zambia	0.858***	3.130***		
	−0.29	−0.95		
Constant	0.0647	−0.059	0.918**	1.555***
	−0.26	−4.58	−0.44	−0.023
Observations	953	953	953	953
$P > Chi^2$	0			

Standard errors in parentheses

The asterisks *, ** and *** denote significant at the 10, 5 and 1% level respectively

Table 5.5 Effect of corruption on process innovation – iv probit estimates

	PROCINN
Reinvested Profits	0.00558***
	−0.0019
Firm Size	0.200**
	−0.09
Highly Educated Manager	0.177***
	−0.049
Highly Educated Workforce	0.00403**
	−0.002
Finance Access Problem	0.0866
	−0.12
Mali	0.604**
	−0.24
Tanzania	−0.586***
	−0.2
Zambia	−0.365
	−0.23
Corruption	0.00329
	−0.013
Constant	−1.473***
	−0.33
Observations	591
$P > chi^2$	0

Standard errors in parentheses
The asterisks *, ** and *** denote significant at the 10, 5 and 1% level respectively

countries, it is the large firms that increase the likelihood to have product innovations. The country dummies were coded with respect to South Africa; therefore, it can be observed that Benin and Zambia are significantly different in product innovations. These results confirm the expectations that corruption is a bigger hindrance to product innovation as the firms have to get the new products into the market and therefore have to face many bureaucratic hurdles in the process. As mentioned in the "sand-the-wheels" hypothesis, this effect stays valid as we can see the negative effect of an imperfect financial market through the financial access variable. Not just financial access but the fact that firms have to rely on their retained profits shows that the pressure of corruption as a cost on investment in innovative activities might be large.

Process Innovation: Because of the acceptance of the Wald test, only probit estimates were used and presented in Table 5.5. As expected, there is no significant effect of corruption on process innovations. Reinvested profits, large firms, highly educated managers, and workforce increase the likelihood of process innovations. Tanzania is likely to produces less process innovations than South Africa while Mali is likely to produces more. This result also confirms the earlier expectations that corruption does not affect activities inside the firm as process innovation does not need a direct usage and requirement of government property. Inherently it is a "within" firm activity.

Table 5.6 Effect of corruption on marketing innovation – instrumental variable probit estimates

| | Instrumented variable | | | |
	MARKINN	Corruption	athrho	lnsigma
Corruption	0.199***			
	−0.05			
Reinvested Profits	−0.00069	0.00657		
	−0.0018	−0.007		
Firm Size	0.218	−0.315		
	−0.18	−0.33		
Client_tech	0.0854	−0.737		
	−0.15	−0.45		
Supp_tech	−0.199	0.402		
	−0.16	−0.43		
Inhousetech	0.149	−0.283		
	−0.14	−0.41		
Highly Educated Manager	0.0682	−0.0828		
	−0.069	−0.17		
High Educated Workforce	0.00268	−0.00847		
	−0.0019	−0.0072		
Finance Access Problem	0.288***	−1.101***		
	−0.11	−0.41		
Mali	−0.302	1.623*		
	−0.26	−0.9		
Tanzania	0.23	−0.203		
	−0.26	−0.79		
Ownership	0.21	−0.731		
	−0.14	−0.54		
Sales to Govt.		−0.0246		
		−0.015		
Efficiency of Govt.		0.0291		
		−0.11		
Faith in Judiciary		−0.114		
		−0.17		
Quality Certification Awarded		0.507		
		−0.34		
Taxes		−0.00667		
		−0.0083		
Constant	−1.614	3.138**	−2.032*	1.477***
	−1.13	−1.54	−1.06	−0.032
Observations	508	508	508	508
$P > chi^2$	0			

Standard errors in parentheses
The asterisks *, ** and *** denote significant at the 10, 5 and 1% level respectively

Marketing Innovation: Table 5.6 presents the instrumental variable probit estimates for marketing innovations. Marketing innovation was measured as whether firms obtained new licensing agreement. In this manner, corruption increases the likelihood

Table 5.7 Effect of corruption on organizational innovation – instrumental variable probit estimates

	ORGINN	Corruption	athrho	lnsigma
Corruption	−0.212***			
	−0.011			
Reinvested Profits	0.00234	0.00813		
	−0.0016	−0.007		
Firm Size	−0.0172	−0.185		
	−0.085	−0.34		
Client_tech	−0.189*	−0.910**		
	−0.1	−0.46		
Supp_tech	0.0137	0.281		
	−0.11	−0.45		
Inhousetech	0.00487	−0.287		
	−0.11	−0.42		
Highly Educated Manager	0.012	−0.11		
	−0.052	−0.18		
High Educated Workforce	−0.00048	−0.00621		
	−0.0019	−0.0073		
Finance Access Problem	−0.289***	−1.383***		
	−0.095	−0.41		
Mali	0.459**	1.421		
	−0.23	−0.92		
Tanzania	−0.0367	−0.214		
	−0.18	−0.79		
Zambia	0.784***	3.504***		
	−0.22	−0.95		
Sales to Govt.		−0.00897		
		−0.0079		
Efficiency of Govt.		0.141		
		−0.12		
Faith in Judiciary		−0.0638		
		−0.09		
Quality Certification Awarded		−0.599		
		−0.41		
Taxes		0.0012		
		−0.0026		
Ownership		−0.173		
		−0.22		
Constant	−0.218	1.948	2.358***	1.517***
	−0.61	−1.24	−0.77	−0.031
Observations	535	535	535	535
$P > \text{chi}^2$	0			

Standard errors in parentheses
The asterisks *, ** and *** denote significant at the 10, 5 and 1% level respectively

of marketing innovation as does the financial access problem. No significant country effects are found. This result is interesting. In one way it can be thought of the support for the "grease-the-wheels" hypothesis. Especially in the context of Africa, it seems to be important to be corrupt to obtain licenses. This can also be thought of an empirical support that obtaining licenses needs corruption. How far is licensing an innovation is a matter of debate. Firms that have a problem with financial access may resort to more licensing in order to increase their market opportunity in the future and may want to use the grant of licenses as a signal to obtain finance.

Organizational Innovation: Table 5.7 presents the instrumental estimation results for organizational innovation. Organizational innovation was measured with respect to the starting of an external joint venture. Corruption decreases the likelihood of organizational innovations, if technology from clients is utilized then it decreases the likelihood too, financial access problem decreases the likelihood to have organizational innovations. Mali and Zambia are significantly different and more likely than South Africa to have organizational innovations. This result too confirms the "sand the wheels" hypothesis, showing that corruption decreases the probability of external relations. One argument that can be posed is that when it comes to external relations one might expect more bureaucratic hurdle especially in societies that are totalitarian or centrally managed. On the other hand, client relationships decrease the likelihood to have an external joint venture. This may be due to cultural reasons and to keep new foreign entrants away from the domestic markets. Imperfect markets also hinder organizational innovation.

5.5 Conclusion

In this paper we presented new arguments of corruption as a sand and grease in the wheel of innovation. We presented arguments on both points of view and propose that what matters inherently is the type of innovation that is in the context and what is the degree of involvement of public property in the given innovative activity. In this manner, we considered four types of innovation, namely – product, process, marketing, and organizational innovation on the basis of the OECD definitions. We proposed that in economies with weak regulatory structures, corruption is more disruptive to innovative activities mainly due to imperfect financial markets, selection of wrong projects by officials due to adverse selection, deliberate delays, decrease investment, and increase in cost of corruption. We also proposed that the "within" firm activity may not be affected by corruption as it does not exclusively use public property. The empirical results on countries in African continent suggest that corruption affects product innovation, process innovation, and organizational innovation negatively and helps improve marketing innovation. This paper has started the process of linking the effect of corruption on growth through innovation. Of course, the paper has its own limitations due to sample size and some definitional issues. Future avenues for research include theoretically linking the triple link of growth–innovation–corruption. This paper contributes both to the literature on public policy and economics of innovation. One of the main aspects of the paper was to give four dimensions of innovation measure and see the effect of corruption on each of this dimension. This method proves useful in showing that it depends on the type of innovation when it comes to analyzing whether corruption is a grease or sand in the wheels of innovation. However, this study is not free of some problems. Mainly the dataset is a cross-section dataset and it would be ideal to use a panel structure, which we are trying to do as part of future research. Explicit elicitation if the firm owns intellectual property would be useful. Also one of the future tasks is to perform the same analysis for all developing countries where corruption is rampant and link that to economic growth models via their effect on innovation. As a first step, this study provides us with useful insights both in terms of theoretical approach to be used in future as well as the kind of results to expect.

Notes

[1] Enterprise Surveys, The World Bank Group. http://www.enterprisesurveys.org/

[2] Throughout the study corruption means bureaucratic corruption, where interaction between public and private actors is the avenue for corruption (see Shleifer & Vishny, 1993 for definition of bureaucratic corruption).

[3] See Méon & Sekkat, 2005 for an empirical test of corruption and growth argued in these lines.

[4] For Transparency international's country wise Corruption Perception Index, visit: http://www.icgg.org

References

Acs, Z. J., & Audretsch, D. B. (1988). Innovation in large and small firms: An empirical analysis. *American Economic Review*, *78*, 678–690.

Acs, Z. J., & Audretsch, D. B. (1990). *Innovation and small firms*. Cambridge: MIT Press.

Aghion, P., Bond, S., Klemm, A., & Marinescu, I. (2004). Technology and financial structure: Are innovative firms different? *Journal of the European Economic Association*, *2*, 277–288.

Alessandrini, P., Presbitero, A. F., & Zazzaro, A. (2008). Banks, distances and firms' financing constraints. *Review of Finance, forthcoming*, 1–47.

Amesse, F., Desranleau, C., Etemad, H., Fortier, Y., & Seguin-Dulude, L. (1991). The individual inventor and the role of entrepreneurship: A survey of the canadian evidence. *Research Policy*, *20*, 13–27.

Anton, J. J., & Yao, D. A. (2002). The sale of ideas: Strategic disclosure, property rights, and contracting. *Review of Economic Studies*, *69*, 513–531.

Anton, J. J., & Yao, D. A. (2004). Little patents and big secrets: Managing intellectual property. *RAND Journal of Economics*, *35*(1), 1–22.

Arrow, K. J. (1962). Economic welfare and the allocation of resources for invention. In R. R. Nelson (Ed.), *The rate and direction of inventive activity*. Princeton, New Jersey: Princeton University Press.

Audretsch, D. B., & Weigand, J. (2005). Do knowledge conditions make a difference?: Investment, finance and ownership in german industries. *Research Policy*, *34*(5), 595–613.

Auken, H. E. V., & Neeley, L. (1996). Evidence of bootstrap financing among small start-up firms. *Journal of Entrepreneurial and Small Business Finance*, *5*, 235–250.

Azoulay, P., Ding, W., & Stuart, T. (2007). The determinants of faculty patenting behavior: Demographics or opportunities? *Journal of Economic Behavior and Organization*, *63*, 599–623.

Baas, T., & Schrooten, M. (2006). Relationship banking and smes: A theoretical analysis. *Small Business Economics*, *27*, 127–137.

Bailey, D. (1966). The effects of corruption in a developing nation. *Western Political Quarterly*, *19*, 719–732.

Baldini, N., Grimaldi, R., & Sobrero, M. (2007). To patent or not to patent? a survey of italian inventors on motivations, incentives, and obstacles to university patenting. *Scientometrics*, *70*, 333–354.

Barton, S. L., & Gordon, P. J. (1987). Corporate strategy: Useful perspective for the study of capital structure? *Academy of Management Review*, *12*, 67–75.

Barton, S. L., & Gordon, P. J. (1988). Corporate strategy and capital structure. *Strategic Management Journal*, *9*, 623–632.

Barton, S. L., & Matthews, C. H. (1989). Small firm financing: Implications from a strategic management perspective. *Journal of Small Business Management*, *27*.

Bates, J. A., & Hally, D. L. (1982). *The financing of small business*. London: Sweet & Maxwell.

Beck, T., DEMIRG-Kunt, A., & Maksimovic, V. (2005). Financial and legal constraints to growth: Does firm size matter? *The Journal of Finance*, *60*(1), 137–177.

Benfratello, L., Schiantarelli, F., & Sembenelli, A. (2006). *Banks and innovation: Microeconometric evidence on italian firms* (Discussion paper No. 2032). Bonn: Institute for the Study of Labor (IZA).

Bercovitz, J., & Feldman, M. (2008). Academic entrepreneurs: Organizational change at the individual level. *Organization Science, 19*, 69.

Berger, A. N., & Udell, G. F. (1995). Relationship lending and lines of credit in small firm finance. *Journal of Business, 68*, 351.

Berger, A. N., & Udell, G. F. (2006). A more complete conceptual framework for sme finance. *Journal of Banking and Finance, 30*, 2945–2966.

Berman, E., Bound, J., & Griliches, Z. (1994). Changes in the demand for skilled labor within us manufacturing: Evidence from the annual survey of manufactures. *Quarterly Journal of Economics, 109*, 367–397.

Bhattacharya, S., & Ritter, J. (1983). Innovation and communication signaling with partial disclosure. *Review of Economic Studies, 50*, 331–346.

Binks, M. R., & Ennew, C. T. (1996). Growing firms and the credit constraint. *Small Business Economics, 8*, 17–25.

Black, S. E., & Strahan, P. E. (2002). Entrepreneurship and bank credit availability. *The Journal of Finance, 57*, 2807–2833.

Blind, K., Edler, J., Frietsch, R., & Schmoch, U. (2006). Motives to patent: Empirical evidence from germany. *Research Policy, 35*(5), 655–672.

Buernstorf, G. (2006). *Is academic entrepreneurship good or bad for science? empirical evidence from the max planck society* (Papers on Economics & Evolution). Jena: Max Planck Institute of Economics.

Carpenter, R. E., & Petersen, B. C. (2002). Capital market imperfections, high-tech investment, and new equity financing. *Economic Journal, 112*(477), F54–F72.

Cassar, G. (2004). The financing of business start-ups. *Journal of Business Venturing, 19*, 261–283.

Chaganti, R., Decarolis, D., & Deeds, D. (1995). Predictors of capital structure in small ventures. *Entrepreneurship: Theory and Practice, 20*.

Chakravarty, S. P. (2006). Regional variation in banking services and social exclusion. *Regional Studies, 40*, 415–428.

Chittenden, F., Hall, G., & Hutchinson, P. (1996). Small firm growth, access to capital markets and financial structure: Review of issues and an empirical investigation. *Small Business Economics, 8*, 59–67.

Cho, I. K., & Kreps, D. M. (1987). Signaling games and stable equilibria. *Quarterly Journal of Economics, 102*, 179–221.

Christensen, J. (2007). The development of geographical specialization of venture capital. *European Planning Studies, 15*, 817–833.

Chung, K. H. (1993). Asset characteristics and corporate debt policy: an empirical test. *Journal of Business Finance & Accounting, 20*, 83–98.

Cohen, W., & Levinthal, D. (1990). Absorptive capacity: A new perspective on learning and innovation. *Administrative Science Quarterly, 35*, 128–152.

Constantinidis, C., Cornet, A., & Asandei, S. (2006). Financing of women-owned ventures: The impact of gender and other owner-and firm-related variables. *Venture Capital-An international journal of entrepreneurial finance, 8*, 133–157.

Cowling, M., & Mitchell, P. (2003). Is the small firms loan guarantee scheme hazardous for banks or helpful to small business? *Small Business Economics, 21*, 63–71.

Davidsson, P. (2006). Nascent entrepreneurship: Empirical studies and developments. *Foundations and Trends in Entrepreneurship, 2*(1), 1–76.

Degryse, H., & Ongena, S. (2005). Distance, lending relationships, and competition. *The Journal of Finance, 60*, 231–266.

Eisenberg, R. S. (1987). Proprietary rights and the norms of science in biotechnology research. *The Yale Law Journal, 97*(2), 177–231.

Elliehausen, G. E., & Wolken, J. D. (1990). Banking markets and the use of financial services by small and medium-sized businesses. *Federal Reserve Bulletin*, *76*, 801.

Engel, D., & Keilbach, M. (2007). Firm-level implications of early stage venture capital investments:an empirical investigation. *Journal of Empirical Finance*, *14*, 150–167.

Etzkowitz, H. (1998). The norms of entrepreneurial science: cognitive effects of the new university industry linkages. *Research Policy*, *27*, 823–833.

European competitiveness report (Tech. Rep.). (2006). Brussels: European Commission.

Fagerberg, J. (1994). Technology and international differences in growth rates. *Journal of Economic Literature*, *32*, 1147–1175.

Faulkender, M., & Petersen, M. A. (2006). Does the source of capital affect capital structure? *Review of Financial Studies*, *19*, 45–79.

Flanigan, J. (2008, April). Despite downturn, financing exists for small companies. *The New York Times*. Available from http://www.nytimes.com/2008/04/17/business/smallbusiness/17edge.html?_r=1

Fraser, S. (2005). *Finance for small and medium-sized enterprises a report on the 2004 uk survey of sme finances*. Warwick: DTI.

Gehrig, T. (1998). Screening, cross-border banking, and the allocation of credit. *Research in Economics*, *52*, 387–407.

Geroski, P. (1994). *Market structure, corporate performance, and innovative activity*. Oxford: Oxford University Press.

Giuri, P., Mariani, M., Brusoni, S., Crespi, G., Francoz, D., Gambardella, A., et al. (2007). Inventors and invention processes in europe: Results from the patval-eu survey. *Research Policy*, *36*, 1107–1127.

Göktepe, D. (2008). *Inside the ivory tower: Inventors & patents at lund university*. Lund: Lund University Press.

Gompers, P., & Lerner, J. (2001). *The money of invention: How venture capital creates new wealth*. Boston, MA: Harvard Business School Press.

Greene, W. H. (2003). *Econometric analysis* (5th ed.). New Jersey: Prentice Hall.

Gulbrandsen, M. (2004). "but peters in it for the money" - the liminality of entrepreneurial scientists. *VEST Journal for Science and Technology Studies*, *18*, 1–22.

Hall, B. H. (2002). The financing of research and development. *Oxford Review of Economic Policy*, *18*(1), 35–51.

Hall, B. H., & Ziedonis, R. M. H. (2001). The patent paradox revisited: Determinants of patenting in the us semiconductor industry, 1980–94. *The RAND Journal of Economics*, *32*(1), 101–128.

Hauswald, R., & Marquez, R. (2006). Competition and strategic information acquisition in credit markets. *Review of Financial Studies*, *19*, 967–1000.

Hayes, L. D. (1999). What the general practitioner should know about patenting business methods. *The Computer Lawyer*, *16*(9), 3–18.

Hellman, T., & Puri, M. (2000). The interaction between product market and financing strategy: the role of venture capital. *Review of Financial Studies*, *13*, 959–984.

Hilal, D. K., & Soltan, H. (1992). To prototype pr not to prototype? that is the question. *Software Engineering Journal*, *7*(6), 388–392.

Horstmann, I., MacDonald, G. M., & Slivinski, A. (1985). Patents as information transfer mechanisms: To patent or (maybe) not to patent. *Journal of Political Economy*, *93*(5), 837–58.

Hsu, D. (2004). What do entrepreneurs pay for venture capital affiliation? *Journal of Finance*, *59*(4), 1805–1844.

Hutchinson, R. W. (1995). The capital structure and investment decisions of the small owner-managed firm: Some exploratory issues. *Small Business Economics*, *7*, 231–239.

Jeon, D. S., & Menicucci, D. (2008). Money, fame and the allocation of talent: Brain drain and the institution of science. *Journal of Economic Behavior and Organization*, *66*, 558–581.

Kamien, M. I., & Schwartz, N. L. (1982). *Market structure and innovation*. Cambridge: Cambridge University Press.

King, R. G., & Levine, R. (1993). Finance and growth: Schumpeter might be right. *The Quarterly Journal of Economics*, *108*(3), 717–37.

Klagge, B., & Martin, R. (2005). Decentralized versus centralized financial systems: is there a case for local capital markets? *Journal of Economic Geography, 5,* 387–421.

Klofsten, M., & Jones-Evans, D. (2000). Comparing academic entrepreneurship in europe:the case of sweden and ireland. *Small Business Economics, 14,* 299–309.

Lach, S., & Schankerman, M. (2008). Incentives and invention in universities. *RAND Journal of Economics, 39*(2), 403–433.

Lawrence, R. Z., & Slaughter, M. J. (1993). International trade and american wages in the 1980s: Giant sucking sound or small hiccup? *Brookings Papers on Economic Activity,* 161–226.

Leff, N. H. (1964). Economic development through bureaucratic corruption. *American Behavioral Scientist, 8,* 8–14.

Leland, H. E., & Pyle, D. H. (1977). Informational asymmetries, financial structure, and financial intermediation. *Journal of Finance, 32*(2), 371–87.

Lemley, A. M. (2001). Rational ignorance at the patent office. *Northwestern University Law Review, 95*(4), 1495–1532.

Levin, R., & Travis, V. (1987). Small company finance: What the books dont say. *Harvard Business Review, 65,* 30–32.

Levin, R. C., Klevorick, A. K., Nelson, R. R., & Winter, S. G. (1987). Appropriating the returns from industrial research and development. *Brookings Papers on Economic Activity*(3), 783–831.

Levin, S. G., & Stephan, P. E. (1991). Research productivity over the life cycle: evidence for academic scientists. *American Economic Review, 81,* 114–132.

Le Vine, V. T. (1975). *Political corruption: The ghana case.* Stanford: Hoover Institution Press.

Long, C. (2002). Patent signals. *The University of Chicago Law Review, 69*(2), 625–679.

Love, J. H., & Roper, S. (1999). The determinants of innovation: R & d, technology transfer and networking effects. *Review of Industrial Organization, 15,* 43–64.

Lui, F. T. (1985). An equilibrium queuing model of bribery. *The Journal of Political Economy, 93,* 760–781.

Macdonald, S. (1984). The patent system and the individual inventor. *The Inventor, 24,* 25–29.

Macdonald, S. (1986). The distinctive research of the individual inventor. *Research Policy, 15*(4), 199–210.

Mankiw, N. G., & Whinston, M. D. (1986). Free entry and social inefficiency. *Rand Journal of Economics, 17,* 48–58.

Markman, G. D., Gianiodis, P. T., Phan, P. H., & Balkin, D. B. (2004). Entrepreneurship from the ivory tower: Do incentive systems matter? *The Journal of Technology Transfer, 29,* 353–364.

Mauro, P. (1995). Corruption and growth. *Quarterly Journal of Economics, 110,* 681–712.

Mbaku, J. M. (1997). *Institutions and reform in africa: the public choice perspective.* Westport, CT: Praeger.

Méon, P. G., & Sekkat, K. (2005). Does corruption grease or sand the wheels of growth? *Public Choice, 122,* 69–97.

Merges, R. P., & Nelson, R. R. (1990). On the complex economics of patent scope. *Columbia Law Review, 90*(4), 839–916.

Merges, R. P., & Nelson, R. R. (1994). On limiting or encouraging rivalry in technical progress: The effect of patent scope decisions. *Journal of Economic Behavior & Organization, 25*(1), 1–24.

Merton, R. K. (1973). The normative structure of science. In R. Merton (Ed.), *R.k.merton,the sociology of science: Theoretical and empirical investigations.* Chicago, IL: University of Chicago Press.

Meyer, M. (2005). Independent inventors and public support measures: insights from 33 case studies in finland. *World Patent Information, 27,* 113–123.

Monfardini, C., & Radice, R. (2008). Testing exogeneity in the bivariate probit model: A monte carlo study. *Oxford Bulletin of Economics and Statistics, 70,* 271–282.

Morck, R., & Yeung, B. (2001). *The economic determinants of innovation* (Tech. Rep. No. 25). Ontario: Industry Canada.

Mowery, D. C. (2006). Universities in national systems of innovation. In J. Fagerber, D. Mowery, & R. Nelson (Eds.), *The oxford handbook of innovation* (p. 209–239). Oxford: Oxford University Press.

Mowery, D. C., & Ziedonis, A. A. (2002). Academic patent quality and quantity before and after the bayh-dole act in the united states. *Research Policy, 31*, 399–418.

Myers, S., & Majluf, N. S. (1984). Corporate financing and investment decisions when firms have information that investors do not have. *Journal of Financial Economics, 13*, 187–221.

Myrdal, G., & Fund, T. C. (1968). *Asian drama: An inquiry into the poverty of nations.* New York, NY: Pantheon.

Nelson, R. R. (1959). The simple economics of basic scientific research. *The Journal of Political Economy, 67*(3), 297–306.

Newey, W. K. (1987). Efficient estimation of limited dependent variable models with endogenous explanatory variables. *Journal of Econometrics, 36*, 231–250.

OECD. (2005). *Oslo manual: Guidelines for collecting an interpreting innovation data* (3rd ed.). Paris: OECD press.

Orser, B. J., Riding, A. L., & Manley, K. (2006). Women entrepreneurs and financial capital. *Entrepreneurship Theory and Practice, 30*, 643–665.

O'Sullivan, M. (2006). Finance and innovation. In J. Fagerber, D. Mowery, & R. Nelson (Eds.), *The oxford handbook of innovation* (p. 240–265). Oxford: Oxford University Press.

Owen-Smith, J., & Powell, W. W. (2003). The expanding role of university patenting in the life sciences: assessing the importance of experience and connectivity. *Research Policy, 32*, 1695–1711.

Owen-Smith, J., Riccaboni, M., Pammolli, F., & Powell, W. W. (2002). A comparison of u.s. and european university-industry relations in the life sciences. *Manage. Sci., 48*(1), 24–43.

Parker, S. C., & Belghitar, Y. (2006). What happens to nascent entrepreneurs? an econometric analysis of the psed. *Small Business Economics, 27*(1), 81–101.

Patti, E. B. di, & Gobbi, G. (2001). The changing structure of local credit markets: Are small businesses special? *Journal of Banking and Finance, 25*, 2209–2237.

Petersen, M. A., & Rajan, R. G. (1995). The effect of credit market competition on lending relationships. *The Quarterly Journal of Economics, 110*(2), 407–43.

Petersen, M. A., & Rajan, R. G. (2002). Does distance still matter? the information revolution in small business lending. *The Journal of Finance, 57*, 2533–2570.

Pollard, J. S. (2003). Small firm finance and economic geography. *Journal of Economic Geography, 3*, 429–452.

Qian, Y., & Xu, C. (1998). Innovation and bureaucracy under soft and hard budget constraints. *The Review of Economic Studies, 65*, 151–164.

Reynolds, P. D., Carter, N. M., Gartner, W. B., & Greene, P. G. (2004). The prevalence of nascent entrepreneurs in the united states: Evidence from the panel study of entrepreneurial dynamics. *Small Business Economics, 23*(4), 263–284.

Riding, A. L., & Swift, C. S. (1990). Women business owners and terms of credit: some empirical findings of the canadian experience. *Journal of Business Venturing, 5*, 327–340.

Romano, C. A., Tanewski, G. A., & Smyrnios, K. X. (2001). Capital structure decision making a model for family business. *Journal of Business Venturing, 16*, 285–310.

Rose-Ackerman, S. (1997). The political economy of corruption. *Corruption and the Global Economy*, 31–60.

Rosenberg, N. (1974). Science, invention and economic growth. *Economic Journal, 84*(333), 90–108.

Rothaermel, F. T., Agung, S. D., & Jiang, L. (2007). University entrepreneurship: a taxonomy of the literature. *Industrial and Corporate Change, 16*(4), 691–791.

Scherer, F. M. (1992). Schumpeter and plausible capitalism. *Journal of Economic Literature, 30*, 1416–1433.

Schmookler, J. (1966). *Invention and economic growth.* Cambridge: Harvard University Press.

Schumpeter, J. A. (1934). *The theory of economic development: An inquiry into profits, capital, credit, interest, and the business cycle* (1949th ed.). Cambridge, MA: Harvard University Press.

Schumpeter, J. A. (1942). *Capitalism, socialism and democracy* (1976th ed.). London: Allen and Unwin.

Shaffer, S. (1998). The winner's curse in banking. *Journal of Financial Intermediation, 7,* 359–392.

Shleifer, A., & Vishny, R. W. (1993). Corruption. *Quarterly Journal of Economics, 108,* 599–617.

Siegel, D. S., & Phan, P. (2005). Analyzing the effectiveness of university technology transfer: implications for entrepreneurship education. *Advances in the Study of Entrepreneurship, Innovation, and Economic Growth, 16,* 1–38.

Siegel, D. S., Waldman, D., & Link, A. (2003). Assessing the impact of organizational practices on the relative productivity of university technology transfer offices: an exploratory study. *Research Policy, 32,* 27–48.

Sirilli, G. (1987). Patents and inventors: An empirical study. *Research Policy, 16,* 157–174.

Slaughter, S., & Leslie, L. L. (1997). *Academic capitalism: Politics, policies, and the entrepreneurial university.* Baltimore: Johns Hopkins University Press.

Spence, M. (1973). Job market signaling. *Quarterly Journal of Economics, 87,* 355–374.

Spence, M. A. (1973). Job market signaling. *The Quarterly Journal of Economics, 87*(3), 355–74.

Stephan, P. E. (1996). The economics of science. *Journal of Economic Literature, 34*(3), 1199–1235.

Stephan, P. E., & Levin, S. G. (2005). Leaving careers in it: Gender differences in retention. *The Journal of Technology Transfer, 30,* 383–396.

Stern, S. (2004). *Biological resource centers: Knowledge hubs for the life sciences.* Washington, D.C: Brookings Institution Press.

Thursby, J., & Thursby, M. (forthcoming). Knowledge creation and diffusion of public science with intellectual property rights. *Intellectual Property Rights and Technical Change, Frontiers in Economics Series, 2.*

Thursby, J. G., Jensen, R., & Thursby, M. C. (2001). Objectives, characteristics and outcomes of university licensing: A survey of major us universities. *The Journal of Technology Transfer, 26,* 59–72.

Ueda, M. (2004). Banks versus venture capital: Project evaluation, screening, and expropriation. *The Journal of Finance, 59,* 601–621.

UNDP. (2001). *Human development report. making new technologies work for human development.* New York: Oxford University Press.

Veracierto, M. (2008). Corruption and Innovation. *Economic Perspectives, 32,* 29–39.

Wilde, J. (2000). Identification of multiple equation probit models with endogenous dummy regressors. *Economics Letters, 69,* 309–312.

Williamson, S. D. (1984). *Costly monitoring, loan contracts and equilibrium credit rationing* (Working Papers No. 572). Ontario,Canada: Queen's University, Department of Economics.

Zazzaro, A. (2002). The allocation of entrepreneurial talent under imperfect lending decisions. *Rivista italiana degli economisti,* 303–330.

Index